Psychotherapy
Integration

Theories of Psychotherapy Series

Theories of Psychotherapy Series

Jon Carlson and Matt Englar-Carlson, Series Editors

Psychotherapy Integration

George Stricker

American Psychological Association

Washington, DC

Published by
American Psychological Association
750 First Street, NE
Washington, DC 20002
www.apa.org

To order
APA Order Department
P.O. Box 92984
Washington, DC 20090-2984
Tel: (800) 374-2721; Direct: (202) 336-5510
Fax: (202) 336-5502;
TDD/TTY: (202) 336-6123
Online: www.apa.org/books/
E-mail: order@apa.org

In the U.K., Europe, Africa, and the Middle East, copies may be ordered from
American Psychological Association
3 Henrietta Street
Covent Garden, London
WC2E 8LU England

Typeset in Minion by Shepherd Inc., Dubuque, IA

Printer: Edwards Brothers, Ann Arbor, MI
Cover Designer: Minker Design, Sarasota, FL
Cover Art: *Lily Rising*, 2005, oil and mixed media on panel in craquelure frame, by Betsy Bauer.

The opinions and statements published are the responsibility of the authors, and such opinions and statements do not necessarily represent the policies of the American Psychological Association.

Library of Congress Cataloging-in-Publication Data

Stricker, George.
  Psychotherapy integration / George Stricker. — 1st ed.
      p. ; cm.
  Includes bibliographical references and index.
  ISBN-13: 978-1-4338-0719-0
  ISBN-10: 1-4338-0719-X
  1. Psychotherapy. I. Title.
  [DNLM: 1. Psychotherapy. WM 420 S9165p 2010]
  RC475.S77 2010
  616.89'14—dc22
                          2009030792

British Library Cataloguing-in-Publication Data
A CIP record is available from the British Library.

Printed in the United States of America
First Edition

To Joan, with whom I have spent the past

To Jocie and Hondo, Geoffery and Laura, who are the present

To Ethan, Jack, Noah, Caroline, and Katherine, who represent the future

Contents

Series Preface

Some might argue that in the contemporary clinical practice of psychotherapy, evidence-based intervention and effective outcome have
overshadowed theory in importance. Maybe. But, as the editors of this
series, we don't propose to take up that controversy here. We do know that
psychotherapists adopt and practice according to one theory or another
because their experience, and decades of good evidence, suggests that having a sound theory of psychotherapy leads to greater therapeutic success.
Still, the role of theory in the helping process can be hard to explain. This
narrative about solving problems helps convey theory's importance:

> Aesop tells the fable of the sun and wind having a contest to decide
> who was the most powerful. From above the earth, they spotted a
> man walking down the street, and the wind said that he bet he could
> get his coat off. The sun agreed to the contest. The wind blew and the
> man held on tightly to his coat. The more the wind blew, the tighter
> he held. The sun said it was his turn. He put all of his energy into
> creating warm sunshine and soon the man took off his coat.

What does a competition between the sun and the wind to remove a
man's coat have to do with theories of psychotherapy? We think this decep-
tively simple story highlights the importance of theory as the precursor to
any effective intervention—and hence to a favorable outcome. Without a
guiding theory, we might treat the symptom without understanding the
role of the individual. Or we might create power conflicts with our clients
and not understand that, at times, indirect means of helping (sunshine)
are often as effective—if not more so—than direct ones (wind). In the
absence of theory, we might lose track of the treatment rationale and
instead get caught up in, for example, social correctness and not wanting
to do something that looks too simple.

What exactly *is* theory? The *APA Dictionary of Psychology* defines theory as "a principle or body of interrelated principles that purports to explain or predict a number of interrelated phenomena." In psychotherapy, a theory is a set of principles used to explain human thought and behavior, including what causes people to change. In practice, a theory creates the goals of therapy and specifies how to pursue them. Haley (1997) noted that a theory of psychotherapy ought to be simple enough for the average therapist to understand, but comprehensive enough to account for a wide range of eventualities. Furthermore, a theory guides action toward successful outcomes while generating hope in both the therapist and client that recovery is possible.

Theory is the compass that allows psychotherapists to navigate the vast territory of clinical practice. In the same ways that navigational tools have been modified to adapt to advances in thinking and ever-expanding territories to explore, theories of psychotherapy have changed over time. The different schools of theories are commonly referred to as waves, the first wave being psychodynamic theories (i.e., Adlerian, psychoanalytic), the second wave learning theories (i.e., behavioral, cognitive–behavioral), the third wave humanistic theories (person-centered, gestalt, existential), the fourth wave feminist and multicultural theories, and the fifth wave postmodern and constructivist theories. In many ways, these waves represent how psychotherapy has adapted and responded to changes in psychology, society, and epistemology as well as to changes in the nature of psychotherapy itself. Psychotherapy and the theories that guide it are dynamic and responsive. The wide variety of theories is also testament to the different ways in which the same human behavior can be conceptualized (Frew & Spiegler, 2008).

It is with these two concepts in mind—the central importance of theory and the natural evolution of theoretical thinking—that we developed the APA Theories of Psychotherapy Series. Both of us are thoroughly fascinated by theory and the range of complex ideas that drive each model.

As university faculty members who teach courses on the theories of psychotherapy, we wanted to create learning materials that not only highlight the essence of the major theories for professionals and professionals in training but also clearly bring the reader up to date on the current status of the models. Often in books on theory, the biography of the original theorist overshadows the evolution of the model. In contrast, our intent is to highlight the contemporary uses of the theories as well as their history and context.

As this project began, we faced two immediate decisions: which theories to address and who best to present them. We looked at graduate-level theories of psychotherapy courses to see which theories are being taught, and we explored popular scholarly books, articles, and conferences to determine which theories draw the most interest. We then developed a dream list of authors from among the best minds in contemporary theoretical practice. Each author is one of the leading proponents of that approach as well as a knowledgeable practitioner. We asked each author to review the core constructs of the theory, bring the theory into the modern sphere of clinical practice by looking at it through a context of evidence-based practice, and clearly illustrate how the theory looks in action.

There are 24 titles planned for the series. Each title can stand alone or can be put together with a few other titles to create materials for a course in psychotherapy theories. This option allows instructors to create a course featuring the approaches they believe are the most salient today. To support this end, APA Books has also developed a DVD for each of the approaches that demonstrates the theory in practice with a real client. Some of the DVDs show therapy over six sessions. Contact APA Books for a complete list of available DVD programs (http://www.apa.org/videos).

One of the major shifts in the past 30 years has been the acceptance and use of integrative models of therapeutic practice. In *Psychotherapy Integration*, Dr. George Stricker showcases various ways of combining the best of different models in contemporary clinical practice. He highlights clinical research to support the efficacy of integrative therapy with numerous populations and conditions. In addition to the focus on evidence-based practice, Dr. Stricker provides extensive case examples that depict how various integrative models, including his own, work from a process perspective. Because of the widespread adoption of this model by practitioners and training programs alike, *Psychotherapy Integration* is an important addition to the series.

—Jon Carlson and Matt Englar Carlson

REFERENCES

Frew, J., & Spiegler, M. (2008). *Contemporary psychotherapies for a diverse world.* Boston: Lahaska Press.

Haley, J. (1997). *Leaving home: The therapy of disturbed young people.* New York: Routledge.

Psychotherapy
Integration

1

Introduction

The great French playwright Molière, in his classic work *Le Bourgeois Gentilhomme*, had one of his characters, Monsieur Jourdain, exclaim, "For more than forty years I have been speaking prose without knowing anything about it! And I am very obliged to you for having taught me that" (Molière, 1670/1957, pp. 34–35). Similarly, many psychotherapists have been practicing psychotherapy integration for many years without being aware that they are doing so. The goal of this text is to introduce students of psychotherapy to psychotherapy integration and to the theory behind this approach. It is important to distinguish between the theory that characterizes many individual approaches to therapy and the meta-theory of integration that leads to a synthesis of some combination of these individual approaches.

With so many different single orientations to psychotherapy (Corsini & Wedding, 2005), no one approach can command a majority of practitioners. However, for decades, the single most frequently endorsed approach has been integrative/eclectic (Norcross, Karpiak, & Lister, 2005). This high percentage of practitioners of psychotherapy integration refers only to declared orientation and probably is an underestimate if many psycho-therapists continue to speak prose without being aware that they are doing so.

If most experienced psychotherapists do practice psychotherapy integration, how is it that the field of psychotherapy integration, virtually unknown as an organized and coherent movement a few decades ago, has become a widely recognized and accepted approach at the present time? A valuable review of this matter (Norcross, 2005) suggests that eight factors are involved:

> 1. Proliferation of therapies; 2. Inadequacy of single theories and treatments; 3. External socioeconomic contingencies; 4. Ascendancy of short-term, problem focused treatments; 5. Opportunity to observe various treatments, particularly for difficult disorders; 6. Recognition that therapeutic commonalities heavily contribute to outcome; 7. Identification of specific therapy effects; 8. Development of a professional network for integration. (p. 5)

Gold (1993) also cites the proliferation of effective psychopharmacological agents, an increased emphasis on biological explanations of psychopathology, and the economic and clinical intrusions of managed care as additional reasons for the increased attention to psychotherapy integration. Whatever the reasons may be, a set of disparate influences has coalesced into a widely recognized movement, an international professional organization, and a quarterly journal in a short period of time. This book will examine what that movement consists of, how it is approached, what theory supports it, and what types of applications have been developed.

Let us begin with a definition. *Psychotherapy integration* includes various attempts to look beyond the confines of single-school approaches to see what can be learned from other perspectives. It is characterized by openness to various ways of integrating diverse theories and techniques. Before beginning to consider the various approaches to psychotherapy integration, it is important to draw several distinctions.

The first distinction is between psychotherapy integration and integrative psychotherapy. An integrative psychotherapy refers to an established but integrated approach to psychotherapy. As such, it may not be anything other than another single school approach. Several integrative psychotherapies have been developed within the psychotherapy integration approach, and we will examine these in due course. However, no single integrative psychotherapy represents the culmination of the psychotherapy integration movement. In contrast, psychotherapy integration characterizes the activity of a psychotherapist who remains open to the contributions of various single schools in working with an individual client. Thus, psychotherapy integration refers to a process by which many different theories and techniques are considered before arriving at a treatment plan and set of treatment activities. In contrast, integrative psychotherapy refers to a product, an established, even if multifaceted, approach to psychotherapy. There is some controversy within the field of psychotherapy integration as to which of these two are preferable: Some people contend there has been sufficient integration and it is time for the field to arrive at an agreed-upon approach, whereas others prefer the focus on process rather than the foreclosure that comes with an agreed-upon approach (Stricker, 1994). I prefer the latter approach and will use it in this volume.

It is easy to confuse psychotherapy integration with an eclectic approach to psychotherapy. An eclectic approach is one in which the therapist chooses interventions because she feels that they work, without the need for a theoretical basis for, understanding of, or necessary concern with the reason for using the technique other than that of apparent efficacy. Psychotherapy integration differs from eclecticism in that it attends to the relationship between theory and technique. It is important to note that the vast majority of practitioners of psychotherapy integration prefer the term *integration to eclecticism* (Norcross et al., 2005) and view integration as a higher-order approach to theory rather than the absence of a guiding theory. The distinction between the two terms is particularly difficult because some important authors who identify with psychotherapy integration also prefer to think of themselves as being eclectic (Beutler, Harwood, Bertoni, & Thomann, 2006; Lazarus, 2005). However, systematization and theory play an important role in each of those approaches, and that seems to move the approaches from eclecticism to psychotherapy integration.

The term *psychotherapy integration* has been used to apply to several distinctive approaches to integration (Stricker & Gold, 2007). Briefly and simply to acquaint the reader with these terms, I will define each of the approaches. The label *psychotherapy integration* has been applied to a common factors approach to understanding psychotherapy, which identifies

those aspects of psychotherapy that are present in most, if not all, therapeutic systems. This term also has been applied to *technical integration*, in
which a combination of techniques is drawn from different therapeutic
systems without regard for any specific theoretical approach. *Theoretical integration*, or an attempt to understand the client by developing a
superordinate theoretical framework that draws from a variety of different frameworks, may be the most difficult to achieve of the approaches to
psychotherapy integration. Finally, *assimilative integration*, which combines
treatments drawn from different approaches but remains guided by a
unitary theoretical understanding, is the most recent addition to the list
of approaches to psychotherapy integration. I prefer assimilative integration and therefore will focus on this approach in this book. This is partly
a matter of personal preference; other authors in the field have made different choices. For that reason, it is important to give the reader a grasp of
the full scope of psychotherapy integration rather than limit the focus to
a personal preference. At the same time, it is important to recognize that
assimilative integration is not simply an idiosyncratic preference but is
recognized as the most recently emerging pathway to psychotherapy integration (Norcross et al., 2005). Each of the approaches to psychotherapy
integration will be elaborated further in a later chapter.

The general point in this cursory presentation of the approaches to
psychotherapy integration is that there generally is a clear value to the
role of theory in psychotherapy integration, whether the theory is the
level at which integration occurs, the framework that governs the choice
of a breadth of technical interventions, or the organizing principle for
understanding the common factors that are present in all psychotherapy.
It also should be recognized that theory is most prominent in theoretical
integration and assimilative integration, plays a lesser role in common
factors, and often may be absent from technical integration.

An additional point must be made before moving to a more full consideration of psychotherapy integration. Psychotherapy may be viewed
as being constituted of a series of theory/technique units. We have seen
that it is possible for integration to occur at the level of theory (theoretical integration), at the level of technique (technical integration), or, more
likely, at both levels (assimilative integration). In considering approaches

to integration, it is important to recognize that theory and technique are separable, so that the presentation of a particular technique in one framework does not preclude its use in another. Similarly, the techniques suggested by a theoretical approach do not present an exhaustive list of possibilities, as other techniques may be introduced. However, although the boundaries between theories and techniques are permeable, shifting a technique from one system to another changes the context in which it is used and, by doing so, changes the meaning and perhaps the utility of the technique.

Finally, it should be noted that the flexibility inherent in psychotherapy integration makes it particularly well suited for dealing with cultural considerations. Any approach that tailors interventions to the needs of individual clients has the ability to adapt those interventions in light of cultural factors, and the wise and empathic practitioner of psychotherapy integration does so.

2

History

It is difficult to pinpoint the provenance of an idea. Change brought about by psychosocial influence has a long and cross-cultural history, a point that underlies some of the most important work in the area of common factors (Frank, 1961). For the purpose of this review, I will restrict the historical account to the history of formal psychotherapy as we know it, which places the starting date for inquiry at about the turn of the 20th century. The point of separation between the origins and the contemporary scene for psychotherapy integration also has an arbitrary quality to it. I will approach this by setting the point of demarcation at 1977, the year of publication of Wachtel's watershed book, *Psychoanalysis and Behavior Therapy*, which ushered in the modern era of psychotherapy integration. Finally, the size of this volume necessarily limits the depth or breadth of a review. The choices I will make are idiosyncratic, perhaps including some works that others will omit and omitting others that are included in other reviews. A more comprehensive recent review (Goldfried, Pachankis, & Bell, 2005) can serve to provide a different but overlapping perspective and a good deal more depth.

ORIGINS

Any review of psychotherapy must start (but not end) with Freud. It is not usual to think of Freud, who often is viewed as doctrinaire and somewhat rigid, as having any connection to psychotherapy integration. However, a careful reading of his cases suggests that Freud was not a Freudian. In explaining his own allegiance to a single form of treatment (psychoanalysis), Freud stated that "there are many ways and means of practicing psychotherapy. All that lead to recovery are good" (Freud, 1905/1953, p. 259). In this same work, he described the psychotherapeutic effect of "expectation colored by faith" (p. 258) and then indicated that "diseases are not cured by the drug but by the . . . personality of the physician" (p. 259). These quotations, aside from presaging the concept of transference, are consistent with the concepts of common factors (expectation, faith) and technical eclecticism (anything effective is good). Thus, seeing Freud as marking the beginning of psychotherapy integration is not as far-fetched as it might seem.

It is more traditional to look to an early contribution by French (1933) as the first work related to psychotherapy integration. In a speech that was not greeted with universal acclaim, French pointed out some similarities between concepts in psychoanalysis, the dominant theory of that time (e.g., repression) and Pavlovian conditioning (e.g., extinction). This would lead to a need to reconcile clinical practice with research findings; it is also an early example of a foundation for theoretical integration. The need to relate psychotherapy integration to the findings of basic research in psychology, hinted at by French's presentation, also is a critical concern for psychotherapy integration.

Rosenzweig (1936) was the first to point out the commonalities in psychotherapy and also coined the use of the term *Dodo bird effect* to refer to the similar results of different approaches to psychotherapy (a finding that underlies the presence of common factors). For Rosenzweig, the common factors were the therapist's personality and ability to inspire hope; interpretations, which provide alternative and more plausible ways of understanding problems, whether or not they are true; and the synergistic effects of one change on others.

Alexander and French (1946), while attempting to introduce a reform within psychoanalysis (and not receiving much credit or approval at the time for doing so), also introduced a pivotal concept in psychotherapy integration. They used the term *corrective emotional experience* to refer to the client being able to re-experience previously difficult relationships in the transferential relationship to the therapist and to solve these difficulties by now being able to experience them in a new way. Thus, for example, problems in relationships with difficult authority figures could be modified by contact with the benign authority of the therapist. Recognizing the value of experiencing old relationships in new ways and then extending this principle beyond the therapy relationship is central to many contemporary approaches to psychotherapy integration (e.g., Stricker & Gold, 2002). In addition, Alexander and French also suggested the then heretical idea that not only might insight lead to change, but change also might lead to insight. This cyclical notion was a central aspect of Wachtel's (1977) important later work.

Dollard and Miller (1950), perhaps echoing French's earlier call for a reconciliation of psychoanalysis and Pavlovian conditioning (French, 1933), wrote an important volume that seemed to translate psychoanalytic concepts into learning theory terms. At one level, this can be seen as an attempt at theoretical integration and was seen as a demonstration of the compatibility of two competing models of behavior. However, by doing so, Dollard and Miller also pointed to some common factors that underlay both approaches to behavior change. Unfortunately, neither the psychoanalytic nor the behavioral community was ready for this advance at that time.

Perhaps the most important single work in the area of common factors was the landmark book by Jerome Frank, first published in 1961 and now in its third edition (Frank & Frank, 1993). In this work, Frank tried to identify commonalities across a wide variety of change processes, including such seemingly diverse efforts as psychotherapy, brainwashing, religious conversion, and placebo effects. As such, this is the most culturally comprehensive of any of the works in psychotherapy integration.

These common factors initially included expectancy for change, arousal of hope, emotional arousal, encouragement of change outside the change process itself, encouragement of self-understanding through interpretations, and a corrective emotional experience. Later modifications focused on dealing with demoralization through restoring morale and increasing self-esteem. The approach to doing this included an emotionally charged healing relationship; a healing setting; a myth based on a rational and credible conceptual scheme to explain symptoms; and a healing ritual. Terms such as *myth* and *ritual* may not seem comfortable for psychotherapists, but they are necessary to indicate commonalities between psychotherapy and other change processes.

It has been commonplace for authors to refer to there being more than 400 schools of psychotherapy; this tally is so well accepted that it is rare for these references to include an attribution for this estimate (for a notable exception, see Corsini & Wedding, 2005). However, in an important deviation from this pattern, London (1964) suggested that there are only two approaches, the action-oriented approach and the insight-oriented approach, and that it would be desirable to integrate these two efforts. Much as the names imply, action-oriented approaches such as behavior therapy encourage the client to take action to change behavior, whereas insight-oriented approaches such as psychodynamic therapy seek to discuss matters of concern to promote understanding. Increasingly, it is becoming clear that most effective and lasting psychotherapeutic change requires both increased understanding and behavior change. In light of the extensive literature on common factors and the lack of clear differences between even the major approaches to psychotherapy (Wampold et al., 1997), it seems unlikely that there can be 400 truly distinctive approaches, and London's classification, cutting across theoretical differences as it does, has much to recommend it.

Up to this time, there were two major contributions to psychotherapy integration. The first was in the area of common factors, principally in the first edition of Frank's important book (Frank, 1961), which suggested that all approaches to psychotherapy worked on the basis of similar principles. The second was a series of attempts to translate one therapeutic language (usually psychoanalysis) into another (usually learning theory). This culminated in the work of Dollard and Miller (1950), who suggested that the major differences between approaches might be linguistic rather than substantive. Both of these contributions emphasized the similarities rather than the differences between existing orientations. An important exception was London's call for an integration of two distinct approaches to psychotherapy (London, 1964). The time was now ripe for a step forward, and in short order, two significant attempts to develop new and integrative solutions were promulgated.

The first of these was Lazarus's multimodal therapy, initially suggested in 1967 and then fully developed in the next decade (Lazarus, 1976). Lazarus referred to his work as *technical eclecticism* and continues to see it as eclectic rather than integrative. However, although it was presented as a work of technical eclecticism, it fits well in the category of assimilative integration, although that term had not yet been coined. This is because multimodal therapy is organized under the general umbrella of social learning theory and incorporates several diverse techniques, primarily from behavior therapy but including a wide range of other approaches as well. Multimodal therapy uses an organizing schema referred to as the BASIC-ID, with the letters in the acronym referring to concerns in the areas of behavior, affect, sensation, imagery, cognition, interpersonal functioning, and drugs/biology. Any concerns that are identified are then addressed with appropriate techniques, whatever their source, in a sophisticated system of interventions.

The most important and frequently overlooked (in the story of psychotherapy integration) contribution was that of Beck, culminating in his presentation (Beck, Rush, Shaw, & Emery, 1979) of cognitive therapy, which now is referred to as cognitive–behavioral therapy (CBT). Beck produced the first fully realized system of theoretical integration by adding the concepts of cognitive science to the well-developed area of behavior therapy. CBT now is regarded as a unique approach to psychotherapy rather than as an integrative effort. It has been so well accepted that the professional society formerly known as the Association for Advancement of Behavior Therapy recently has been renamed the Association for Behavioral and

Cognitive Therapies. It is the best example of an integrative therapy, as opposed to an effort to maintain a process of psychotherapy integration. Interestingly, as we shall see, many current integrative efforts regard CBT as a primary school of therapy and attempt to integrate aspects of CBT with other approaches to psychotherapy. I will follow this pattern and regard CBT as a single well-defined approach to psychotherapy, but we should not lose sight of its integrative origins.

Despite being identified with psychoanalysis, Marmor continued in the tradition established by French (1933) and Alexander (1963) by looking carefully at the relationship between psychoanalysis and learning theory (Marmor, 1969, 1971). He recognized that basic learning principles occur in all psychotherapy and concluded that the two approaches should not be viewed as competing views of human functioning but rather be seen as complementary. His view of the complexity of human beings called for the insights of both approaches and recognized that some clients might be better suited for one approach than the other. This attempt to seek commonalities between psychoanalysis and behavior therapy was echoed by several other investigators (Beier, 1966; Feather & Rhodes, 1972; Marks & Gelder, 1966), each of whom understood that the two approaches, often seen as in conflict by single school practitioners, had areas of distinct overlap. In particular, the interaction between behavior and unconscious processes, each of which influenced the other, was noted.

EVOLUTION TO THE PRESENT

The contemporary era of psychotherapy integration was marked by the publication of a landmark book by Wachtel, *Psychoanalysis and Behavior Therapy* (1977). The importance of this book lay in its theoretical and technical synthesis of behavior therapy and psychoanalysis. Behavior change was seen as influencing insight and insight as influencing behavior change in a cyclical process that did not have either element as the necessary first point of entry. The movement to a cyclical rather than a linear conception of human processes was an important step forward, and one that has been echoed in many other approaches to psychotherapy integration since then. The integration of behavior therapy and psychoanalysis also led to the necessity for a seamless process of integration, again a need that has been emphasized by many subsequent investigators. The book now has had a second edition (Wachtel, 1997) that carries the integration one step further by also including systems theory in the grand integration that is attempted.

Shortly thereafter, Goldfried (1980) published an influential article that expanded on the area of common factors. Rather than seeking common factors at the level of technique, which clearly was disparate among approaches, or at the level of theory, where very different concepts and worldviews dominated, Goldfried suggested looking at the intermediate level of clinical strategies. These strategies included such processes as providing feedback and corrective emotional experiences and seemed to be a conflict-free zone that might provide ripe ground for rapprochement.

The important works of Wachtel (1977) and Goldfried (1980) set the stage for the establishment of a professional organization that promised to provide a reference group for the growing number of professionals who were interested in psychotherapy integration. The Society for the Exploration of Psychotherapy Integration (SEPI) was established in 1983 and has grown into an international organization that hosts an annual conference and publishes the *Journal of Psychotherapy Integration*, a quarterly journal that offers the most current contributions to the area of psychotherapy integration (for further information about SEPI, see http://www.sepiweb.com).

The transtheoretical approach (Prochaska & DiClemente, 2005) has proven to be an active and valuable set of contributions to psychotherapy integration since the early 1980s. It can be classified as part of theoretical integration because it establishes a metatheory of the psychotherapeutic process. The approach looks at the process of treatment and then, within it, coordinates the various processes, stages, and levels of change. The choice of interventions then varies as a function of these factors, providing a basis of matching that is akin to the system Beutler (Beutler & Clarkin, 1990) would later propose. Of these factors, perhaps the most influential has been the stages of change, which include the precontemplative, the contemplative, preparation, action, and maintenance. Clients in the precontemplative stage of change are not yet open to active efforts at change and have to be moved to contemplative, where they are willing to think about it, and preparation, where they are ready to act, before action attempts are likely to be successful. Regardless of one's orientation to treatment, this is a valuable system to understand and implement.

The attempts to integrate behaviorism and psychoanalysis, which marked many of the efforts to achieve integration, received an important caution (Messer & Winokur, 1984) on the grounds that it was difficult to integrate approaches that had conflicting worldviews and visions of life. For example, if one approach is predicated on the principle that change is accomplished easily and the other posits the great difficulty of meaningful change, how are the two to be combined? Messer (2006) began to answer his own question by noting the extent to which the schools had begun to incorporate the views of the other (a much more abstract level of integration), with the contrasting visions allowing for a fuller vision of the client.

The second major approach to technical eclecticism (after Lazarus) was represented by the work of Beutler, whose system is referred to as prescriptive psychotherapy. This system was first presented in 1990 (Beutler & Clarkin, 1990). The emphasis in prescriptive psychotherapy is on treatment matching; it draws heavily on research to select the interventions that are best suited for particular client presentations. This emphasis on the particular client, which is present in most of the systems of psychotherapy integration, allows for the acknowledgment of cultural difference and the tailoring of treatment to the unique needs of the individual. It is in sharp contrast to an approach that is based on categorization, such as diagnosis, and that is more uniform in application.

We have seen that, of the approaches to psychotherapy integration, common factors was presented first (Frank, 1961), followed by technical eclecticism (Lazarus, 1976) and theoretical integration (Wachtel, 1977). The remaining approach to psychotherapy integration, assimilative integration, was introduced by Messer (1992). Assimilative integration retains allegiance to a single theoretical school but then introduces techniques drawn from other schools, integrated in as seamless a way as possible. The variant of assimilative integration that I have been associated with is referred to as *assimilative psychodynamic psychotherapy integration* (Gold & Stricker, 2001; Stricker & Gold, 2002; Stricker, 2006a), and it will be elaborated further in the next chapter.

One indication of the maturity of a field of study is represented by the presence of a handbook that brings together the major contributors to summarize the developments in that field. For psychotherapy integration, this occurred in the early 1990s with the publication of two such handbooks: *Handbook of Psychotherapy Integration* (Norcross & Goldfried, 1992) and *Comprehensive Handbook of Psychotherapy Integration* (Stricker & Gold, 1993). These books have recently been revised, with one having a second edition (Norcross & Goldfried, 2005a) and the other being converted into a casebook that illustrates the clinical application of the various approaches (Stricker & Gold, 2006a). These four volumes, particularly the most recent editions, offer an expanded summary of the current state of the field for the interested reader. It is of interest to note that our casebook (Stricker & Gold, 2006a) includes illustrations of many of the familiar and standard approaches to psychotherapy integration, but it also includes some novel contributions. These include the integration of humanistic and experiential methods (Watson, 2006), philosophical and epistemological principles (Anchin, 2006), and political and cultural variables (Consoli & Chope, 2006).

Another major approach to psychotherapy integration, but one often not recognized as belonging under the umbrella of integration, is dialectical behavior therapy (DBT). This approach was developed by Linehan (Heard & Linehan, 2005) and, in the spirit of a dialectic, integrates Eastern and Western approaches to psychotherapy. DBT combines many traditional behavioral interventions with promoting the mindfulness associated with the Zen tradition. DBT was initially developed for the treatment of borderline personality disorder, a serious and complex disorder that had proven intractable to previous attempts at treatment. One of the key dialectics expounded within DBT is the conundrum represented by affirming the value of the efforts of the client while still exhorting him to change. Indeed, this is a difficulty within any approach to therapy that values an accepting therapeutic stance and simultaneously seeks to promote change.

One of the most promising of the newer approaches to psychotherapy integration has been referred to as client-directed (and/or outcome-informed) therapy (Duncan, Sparks, & Miller, 2006; Miller, Duncan, & Hubble, 2005). This has been classified within common factors, but if it continues to grow and receive research support, as it has to date (e.g.,

Lambert, Harmon, Slade, Whipple, & Hawkins, 2005), it may well end up being viewed as an approach in its own right. In this approach, no standard theoretical framework is adopted, but rather, the therapy is guided by the client's preferences and theory of change, supplemented by the results of the outcome of this process, so that a failure to achieve results will necessarily lead to a change in interventions. This approach is particularly likely to be responsive to the cultural preferences of the client.

Accelerated experiential dynamic psychotherapy (Fosha, 2002) is a significant new contribution because of the emphasis on affect rather than on behavior or cognition, the previous key foci of change efforts. Psychodynamic understanding and interventions are combined with affect-arousing procedures, more associated with humanistic approaches, in order to promote change. Many of the approaches within psychotherapy integration have taken to emphasizing the importance of affect as a necessary part of any attempt to induce change, and this particular work places affect front and center in its procedures.

Finally, a sophisticated new approach to anxiety disorders (Wolfe, 2005) has accomplished a theoretical integration of theories of anxiety and then combined these with an integrated set of interventions that follow from this new integrated theoretical formulation. Although Wolfe has written this as an approach specific to anxiety disorders and bases it on an integrated conception of anxiety, his general approach has important ramifications that go beyond anxiety. According to Wolfe, the first step in therapy is to address the symptoms that are presented (in this case, anxiety) and then, if the client wishes, to go beyond that to deal with the self-wounds that underlie those symptoms. The general approach of aiding in the remission of symptoms, a more behavioral approach, and then dealing with any personality issues that exist, a more psychodynamic approach, is a good model that can generalize to many more presenting issues than anxiety.

CONTEMPORARY APPROACHES

At the present time psychotherapy integration is organized into four distinct and separable approaches, as has been indicated previously. These approaches, in order of their identification and development, are common factors, technical identification, theoretical integration, and assimilative integration. However, it may be that this existing classification system has exhausted its value and that we are on the verge of an integration of integrative approaches (Stricker & Gold, 2006b). The lines between various approaches are increasingly becoming muddied and classification is becoming more problematic. The true value of determining whether the work of Lazarus, for example, is technical integration, as he prefers, or assimilative integration, as I view it, may be nonexistent, and it is sufficient to know that a creative approach to psychotherapy has been developed without slavish adherence to a theoretical framework and with particular regard to the needs of the clients being served. It may be in this accomplishment that the lasting contribution of psychotherapy integration lays, and not in any arbitrary classification system that may be developed. Nonetheless, it is valuable to review the classification system that has developed because it is pervasive in the field. Before doing so, however, it should be noted that psychotherapy integration is a general approach that is particularly suited to taking cultural factors into account because of the tailoring of interventions to the individual client rather than to an overarching theory.

Common Factors

Common factors refers to an aspect of psychotherapy that is present in most, if not all, approaches to treatment. This collection of universally applied techniques can be seen regardless of the theoretical approach (or lack of same) that is applied; because it is common to all of them, we have assigned the name *common factors* to this variation of psychotherapy integration. It was first identified by Rosenzweig (1936) and discussed by several theorists, most notably by Goldfried and Padawer (1982), who referred to common strategies rather than factors. This area was presented most impressively by Frank (1961), whose work was particularly sensitive to cultural issues, as it looked at common factors across change processes in general, as they occur in multicultural settings. It is likely that beginning therapists adhere to a single fixed system, as that is what they typically have been taught, but that, with increasing experience, they begin to expand their repertoire (Fiedler, 1950) and move closer to psychotherapy integration, whether or not they name it as such. This may be because of the several common aspects of all successful psychotherapy. Most experienced therapists are aware of this common core of nonspecific factors; as a result, we can expect that more experienced therapists will make greater use of the common factors than novices.

Although there is no fixed, established list of common factors, consensus suggests that such a list would include a therapeutic alliance; exposure of the client to prior difficulties followed by a new corrective emotional experience; expectations by the therapist and by the client for positive change; beneficial therapist qualities such as attention, empathy, and positive regard; the provision to the client of a rationale for problems; and the use of some systematic therapeutic procedures or rituals (Grencavage & Norcross, 1990).

Each of these elements is present in almost every variation of psychotherapy that is practiced. Every approach to treatment begins with the establishment of a therapeutic alliance. The therapist and the client agree to work together, agree on goals toward which they will work, and feel jointly committed to a process of change occurring in the client (Bordin, 1979). The approach to forming the alliance, the role of the alliance as a foundation or an integral part of the treatment, and the techniques used to encourage the development of an alliance may vary, but without the joint commitment to the effort and bond between the participants, there can be no successful treatment. Additionally, in almost every approach to treatment, the second of the common factors that has been mentioned, the exposure of the client to prior difficulties, is present. In some instances, such as in variants of behavior therapy, the exposure is in vivo, as a client may be asked directly to confront the source of the difficulties. In many cases, such as the more expressive and psychodynamic treatments, the exposure is verbal and in imagination. However, in every imaginal approach, clients must express their difficulties in some manner and, by doing so, are experiencing those difficulties again through this verbal exposure. In order for the treatment to be successful, the exposure often is followed by a new corrective emotional experience (Alexander & French, 1946). The corrective emotional experience refers to a situation in which an old difficulty is re-experienced in a new and more benign way. As the client learns to re-experience the problem in a new way, it is possible to master that problem and move on to a higher level of adjustment. This corrective emotional experience may occur primarily in the transference, as Alexander and French initially posited, or outside the session, as more recent theorists have emphasized (Stricker, 2006a; Wachtel, 1997), or in both places, as is typical of many attempts at psychotherapy integration.

Within the therapeutic alliance that has been established and when the exposure to difficult situations occurs, it is always in a situation in which both the therapist and the client expect positive change to occur. Faith and hope are common factors that are integral to the change process that occurs in successful therapy. Absent any therapist expectation that change will occur, it is unlikely that she can deliver an effective intervention, and if the client does not have some expectation of change occurring, it is unlikely that any intervention will be successful. Moving to another common factor, there must be beneficial therapist qualities, much as Rogers (1957) posited, such as attending to the client, empathizing with the client's predicament and circumstances, and having and demonstrating a positive regard for the client. Finally, among the common factors, the client is provided with a rationale for the problems that are being experienced. The rationale is derived from the therapist's theory of personality and psychotherapy. The same client may go to several different therapists and may be provided with several different rationales for the same problem. This forces us to consider the interesting question as to whether the rationale that is provided must be correct or whether it is sufficient simply that the rationale is credible to the client. If credibility is sufficient and the client is given a way of understanding what before had been beyond comprehension, we need not get into the problems posed by the search for ultimate truth through theoretical formulations. The central role of culture in the common factors approach is clearest in the landmark work of Frank (1961), who went well beyond psychotherapy to consider all change processes cross-culturally to derive his list of common factors.

A recent and clever approach to organizing the common factors (Weinberger, 1993, 1995) used the acronym REMA to capture the process. In this formulation, the key aspects were relationship, exposure, mastery, and attribution. First, a relationship is formed, and then the client is exposed to the presenting problems (either in vivo or through verbal expression). Next, mastery occurs when the client is able to deal more successfully with the problem, and attribution is the rationale that is given for the problem. Although these processes typically occur sequentially, it is important to understand that they do not form a linear process; there can be feedback among the elements in a cyclical and recurring manner.

Several systems of psychotherapy have been based on a common factors approach. Perhaps the best known of these is Garfield's (1992) integrative therapy, which is based on a common factors notion and relies on insight, exposure, the provision of new experience, and the provision of hope through the therapeutic relationship. Another prominent common factors approach is that of Beitman (Beitman, Soth, & Good, 2006), which looks at the future as the organizing common factor for all clients. Finally, client-directed (and/or outcome-informed) therapy (Duncan et al., 2006; Miller et al., 2005), which I have described previously as a promising new approach, also is seen as a common factors approach, with the theory of the client being the organizing common factor.

Technical Integration

Technical integration refers to the use of techniques drawn from several different therapeutic approaches. It is the approach to psychotherapy integration that is most easily confused with eclecticism. When there is no systematic basis other than the idiosyncratic preferences of the therapist, I prefer to refer to it either as eclecticism or syncretism. When there is a systematic reason for the use of these techniques, technical integration is the preferred term. If technical integration is to be regarded as a meaningful approach to psychotherapy integration rather than a hodgepodge of interventions, it must be distinguished from syncretism. Syncretism refers to a combination of techniques without benefit of any systematic rationale for doing so. It is based on therapist preference and intuition. Where there is a systematic basis for the combination of techniques, technical integration is a valid and important approach to psychotherapy integration. We can take a cue from Rotter (1954), whose work provided the foundation for the thought of Lazarus, in saying that the primary issue is whether to be consistent and systematic, and not whether to be eclectic. For technical integration, where interventions are chosen on the basis of client needs, the ability to take culture into account is clear.

The first major contribution in this area was by Lazarus (1976), who coined the term *technical eclecticism*, although this is now more commonly referred to as technical integration by everyone but Lazarus, who continues to use his original terminology. The acronym that organizes his work, as has been noted previously, is the BASIC-ID. This represents a comprehensive view of human functioning and suggests the thorough and systematic approach that Lazarus takes within the rubric of technical integration.

Since the initial presentation of technical integration, other noteworthy contributions have been made. Foremost among these is that of Beutler (Beutler & Clarkin, 1990), who draws on research as the basis for prescriptive psychotherapy, his systematic approach to technical diversity. He has identified several dimensions of client distinctions, each of which has a corresponding element of therapeutic intervention. For example, a more complex, chronic, and disabling set of presenting problems will require a more elaborate and intensive approach to treatment, and may prove more resistant to change efforts. Clients who are more internalizing and reactant (resistant) are more likely to be responsive to approaches that are less directive, such as can be seen in psychodynamic treatment. Clients who are more externalizing and less reactant will take direction well and are better suited for more cognitive and behavioral approaches to treatment. A therapist using prescriptive psychotherapy will look very different from client to client, but the unifying aspect for that therapist is a clear and systematic approach to choosing how to be different.

Theoretical Integration

Theoretical integration is the most difficult level at which to achieve integration, for it requires bringing together concepts from disparate approaches, some of which may differ in their fundamental worldview (Messer & Winokur, 1980). The blending of approaches that may appear to differ significantly requires a good deal of creativity and has much to offer, but also has many obstacles to successful accomplishment. Assimilative integration, which will be discussed next, begins with the therapist's home theory and then brings together techniques from different theoretical approaches. Theoretical integration, however, tries to bring together those theoretical approaches themselves and to develop what in physics is referred to as a "grand unified theory." Physicists, to my knowledge, have not been successful in producing a grand unified theory and neither have psychotherapists. It is difficult to imagine a theory that can successfully combine a theory that has one worldview with a different theory that has a different worldview. Messer (Messer & Winokur, 1984) has written very well about this problem and has characterized a psychodynamic approach as being tragic and a behavioral approach as being comic. These differences represent a fundamental incompatibility between theoretical worldviews. He is using these words, tragic and comic, as they are used in literary criticism and not in the manner that immediately occurs to the usual reader. He thinks of psychodynamic approaches as being tragic because they focus on an early difficulty leading to a pattern of behavior that is repetitive, destructive, and impossible to resolve. There also is an ironic element involved because, as hard as clients work to overcome their early problems, they often continue to experience the ramifications of that difficulty. Behavior therapy, on the other hand, views problems as much more amenable to change; it is the happy ending to behavior therapy that resembles the comic approach to literary theory. The important point here is that theoretical integration somehow must reconcile a theory about the stability of behavior with a theory about the ready changeability of behavior; unless this obstacle can be overcome, theoretical integration will not be achieved. The recent movement of the separate theories to a point where they resemble each more than they did previously may be a step in this direction. However, theoretical integration remains an elusive holy grail, one that offers significant rewards, but not a level at which most practitioners can function at the present time.

The primary example of theoretical integration is the one developed by Wachtel (1977, 1997), which is of historical as well as psychological importance. This is because it marked the introduction to the contemporary field of psychotherapy integration and created the underpinning for the current state of the art. Wachtel's approach is referred to as cyclical psychodynamics, and with it, he created an integrative relational psychotherapy. Wachtel (1977) accomplished the theoretical integration of psychoanalysis and behavior therapy and, in the most recent version, also of these two with systems theory (Wachtel, 1997). The inclusion of systems theory in the formulation also emphasizes that the client is much more sensitive to external influence and cultural considerations. Cyclical psychodynamics is heavily rooted in relational psychodynamic psychotherapy but also draws on behavioral concepts such as reinforcement, social learning approaches, and, most recently, systems theory. Cognitive and experiential concepts also are included in this ambitious undertaking.

A key concept in cyclical psychodynamics is a vision of directionality in causation as being cyclical rather than linear, so that changes in unconscious motivation can affect behavior (as would be recognized in any psychodynamic theory), changes in behavior can affect unconscious processes (an expansion of the potential impact of interventions aimed at behavior change), and both can affect relationships with others (adding a systems dimension to the approach), which, in turn, affect both. Unlike more traditional psychodynamic approaches, there is an emphasis on current experience rather than an emphasis on past history. This leads to a focus on how current patterns, even if derived from past experience, are being maintained by current relationship patterns. This also introduces the possibility of enactments occurring and the value of the corrective emotional experience in undoing these enactments.

There are several other good and impressive examples of theoretical integration. These include cognitive–analytic therapy (Ryle & Low, 1993), unified psychotherapy (Allen, 2003), and behavioral psychotherapy (Fensterheim, 1993). Cognitive–analytic therapy, as the name implies, blends an object relations approach to psychotherapy with cognitive–behavioral therapy. Unified psychotherapy is one of the few approaches (until Wachtel's recent work) to attempt an integration of psychodynamic therapy with systems theory. Behavioral psychotherapy is an attempt to blend psychodynamic and behavioral work, but unlike the efforts of Wachtel and

Ryle, it begins with a behavioral rather than a psychodynamic foundation. These are all attempts to reach an integrative therapy with a broader base and a more far-reaching and inclusive theoretical approach than any more traditional single school therapy.

Assimilative Integration

Assimilative integration is the most recently developed of the accepted approaches to psychotherapy integration. It is an approach in which a solid grounding in one theoretical position is accompanied by a willingness to incorporate techniques from other therapeutic approaches. The distinction between assimilative integration and technical integration is the consistent use of a single theoretical framework in the former, as opposed to a more loose and varied approach to theory in the latter. In both assimilative integration and technical integration, the activity of the therapist must be tailored to the specific needs of the individual client. However, in doing this within the framework of assimilative integration, an understanding of the client is essential, and theory is used to provide that understanding. In assimilative integration, theory is used initially to help in the understanding of the needs of the client, but then several different approaches to technique, derived from other theoretical frameworks, can help to construct an individualized treatment plan that is consistent with the theoretical understanding. Of course, the treatment plan then must undergo continuous revision because the theoretical understanding of the client becomes more fully developed over the course of the treatment. The various techniques then must be seamlessly blended within the context of understanding provided by the theoretical approach that is integral to the assimilative viewpoint. Culture is always taken into account in the choice of techniques.

Assimilative psychodynamic integration (Gold & Stricker, 2001; Stricker & Gold, 2002; Stricker, 2006a) will be presented in elaborate detail in the next chapter. Other approaches to assimilative integration may include the work of Lazarus (2005), which is organized around social learning theory, and the work of Wolfe (2005), which is based on a humanistic–experiential view of human functioning. However,

Lazarus prefers to see his work as technical integration, and Wolfe easily may be classified within theoretical integration, as his work is built on a platform of a sophisticated blend of theoretical approaches to the anxiety disorders. In addition, cognitive–behavioral assimilative integration (Castonguay, Newman, Borkovec, Grosse Holtforth, & Maramba, 2005) is described as an assimilative theory, although it also may be viewed as sequential rather than assimilative therapy. In this approach, a session of cognitive–behavioral treatment is followed by a session of psychodynamic treatment for the same client, and each is able to synergize the impact of the other. However, each is practiced in a relatively pure manner, so the assimilation occurs in the overall package rather than with a single unified approach to psychotherapy.

If one were an observer of a psychotherapy session, it would be difficult to tell the difference between the various approaches that have been defined here. The blending of various techniques is common to all approaches, and the distinction lies in the mind of the psychotherapist. It is the reasons for the blend rather than the actual techniques employed that distinguish the approaches, and the nature and role of theory is the key distinction.

In our shifting historical account of psychotherapy integration, we have seen the gradual development of the field. Initially, common factors were studied (Frank, 1961; Rosenzweig, 1936), and this was followed by technical integration (Lazarus, 1976). However, the term *psychotherapy integration* was not yet a common one. This awaited the development of theoretical integration (Wachtel, 1977), which ushered in the formal psychotherapy integration movement. The next development was assimilative integration (Messer, 1992), which initially was a theoretical suggestion and later developed into a widely accepted branch of psychotherapy integration. In this time of shifting and expanding definitions, where can we look for the next addition to the realm of psychotherapy integration? My guess is that it may lie with client-directed approaches (Miller et al., 2005), an approach that is less bound by theory and thus may resemble technical integration, but is systematized by the presence of the client as an organizing factor (a common factor, perhaps?).

3

Theory

Up to this point, psychotherapy integration has been viewed as a process rather than a fixed approach, and a survey of various ways of tackling the process have been reviewed. There is no single overall theory that embraces all of psychotherapy integration, but a metatheory asserts that, in the absence of a grand unified theory, there must be an openness and willingness to balance many theoretical and technical approaches to best serve the client. Because clients differ in personality, presenting problems, needs, and cultural background, therapists must be willing to alternate between approaches to provide the best and most suitable services.

At this time, however, I will focus on a single approach within the vast riches afforded by psychotherapy integration, and I have chosen assimilative psychodynamic integration (Gold & Stricker, 2001; Stricker & Gold, 2002; Stricker, 2006a) as the approach that will be developed in greatest detail. As has been outlined previously, this approach relies on a relational psychodynamic theory as the organizing principle but then assimilates many different technical interventions drawn from cognitive, behavioral, experiential, and systems approaches, as they may be helpful.

The psychodynamic approach that is taken is the newer, two-person relational model (Mitchell, 1988) rather than the more classical one-person model, and with this choice, much emphasis is placed on the therapeutic relationship. It is interesting to note that relational psychoanalysis itself is integrative within the psychodynamic area, as it incorporates many earlier models, including object relations, attachment theory, and self-psychology. The key difference separating relational from earlier models of psychoanalytic thinking is in the conception of the content of the unconscious, with more emphasis placed on interpersonal sources than biological ones. For this reason, the distinction between a two-person and a one-person model is made. The emphasis is both on the two people required for the development of an individual, who develops based on interpersonal rather than one-person biological forces, and also on the activity required of both participants in the therapeutic relationship, rather than the more silent blank screen of the one-person approach.

The critical notion of assimilation requires that a single theoretical model—in this case relational psychoanalysis—makes use of techniques developed by other approaches to psychotherapy. The failure of the central model to suggest these techniques then requires some accommodation, or the alteration of the base theory to include the possibility of using these techniques in a manner consistent with the larger theory. The accommodation that we have developed is called the three-tier model of psychotherapy and personality (Gold & Stricker, 1993; Stricker & Gold, 1988). Although the model was developed within the context of assimilative psychodynamic integration, it is widely applicable because of the comprehensiveness of the approach.

The three tiers can be conceptualized as a triangle divided longitudinally into three sections. The top section, Tier 1, is concerned with behavior. The middle section, Tier 2, deals with cognition, affect, perception, and sensation. The base of the triangle, Tier 3, includes unconscious processes, including images, representations of others, motives, and conflicts. Consistent with our psychodynamic orientation, emphasis is placed on the foundational Tier 3, but a great deal more recognition and attention is

Figure 3.1

The Three-Tier Model of Functioning

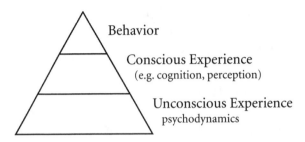

Behavior

Conscious Experience
(e.g. cognition, perception)

Unconscious Experience
psychodynamics

given to the other tiers, including an important conception of the inter-relatedness of the tiers. Thus, behavior and conscious experience are not simply derivatives of unconscious processes but are important in and of themselves. Because each of the tiers relates to the other two, causality is not linear from the bottom up, as in a traditional psychodynamic model, but is cyclical, with each tier reverberating within the others. A graphic picture of the three tiers is presented in Figure 3.1.

As an example of this conceptual scheme, behavior (Tier 1) is motivated and shaped by unconscious factors (Tier 3) and also determined by conscious perceptions and appraisals of the situation (Tier 2). However, changes in behavior can lead to changes in conscious perceptions and also can lead to changes in the structure of unconscious representations of the event. The implication of this circularity is that the point of entry does not matter, because change in any tier can lead to change in the others. Thus, we will examine unconscious processes and strive to help the client to understand them, as in traditional psychodynamic work. However, we also will be comfortable assigning homework to alter behavior (Tier 1) and suggesting a rethinking of constructions of others (Tier 2), confident that these will have an impact on the unconscious processes (Tier 3) that previously had been seen as necessary to approach directly and solely.

GOALS

The goal of psychotherapy integration, most generally, is to help the client to improve. The nature of the improvement depends on the particular variant of psychotherapy integration that is being practiced. In some cases the improvement is in behavior (Tier 1), in some cases it is in affect (Tier 2), and in others it is in understanding (a Tier 2 reflection of a Tier 3 accomplishment). In all cases, the specific goals should be determined through a joint consultation process between the therapist and the client. In some cases, it is important to distinguish between the overt goals of the client, such as behavior change, and the more covert, process goals of the therapist, such as the understanding that might be seen as necessary to achieve the behavior change. Even if the latter is so, it would behoove the therapist to explain that to the client, so that the therapist's lines of inquiry will seem to the client to be rational and goal-directed.

The predominant theory in the integrative model often determines the focus of the treatment. If the theory is behavioral, the goals are likely to be behavioral. In cognitive–behavioral treatment, the goals also are behavioral, but the process goals include cognitive change. In experiential therapy, the goals are more likely to be affective, whereas in psychodynamic work, understanding often is the key, either for the client as an end product or for the therapist as a means to an end for the client. Within our assimilative approach, each of these is recognized as important, although the relative importance will vary with the presenting problems and concerns of the client. We also have seen that there are approaches in which the view of the client is placed foremost (Miller, Duncan, & Hubble, 2005), and the goals and theories of change are determined almost exclusively by the client, independent of the predilections of the therapist.

The most general statement that can be made about goals in psychotherapy integration is that the goals are idiographic rather than nomothetic. Each treatment is tailored to the needs of the individual client, and as a result, each treatment will pursue a different set of goals as determined by the client. The therapist will determine the processes and strategies necessary to reach those goals, but the goals themselves are established jointly with the client.

The full range of concerns of psychotherapy integration is captured best by a mnemonic that I have devised for teaching purposes. It quite simply is ABCDEF. The meaning of these terms is:

Affect

Behavior

Cognition

Dynamics

Environment

Fysiology

This bears some overt resemblance to the ABC of rational emotive therapy (Ellis, 1962), although, for Ellis, the letters refer to activating event, belief, and emotional consequence. My mnemonic also is reminiscent of the BASIC-ID of multimodal therapy (Lazarus, 2005). However, Ellis does not attend to much beyond the cognitive processes of the client, and Lazarus, who is much more comprehensive, purposely excludes any reference to the unconscious, as captured by the concept of dynamics.

It is apparent that many of the single school approaches focus on one or the other of these key concerns. Affect is the province of humanistic treatment, behavior of behavior therapy, cognition of cognitive therapy, dynamics of psychodynamic therapy, environment of systems approaches, and physiology of psychopharmacology. As a peripheral note, when I was reluctant to engage in the cuteness of fysiology, I thought of using F for family and G for genes. However, genes represent a small portion of what is determined by physiological processes and family does seem to be covered by environment, so I reluctantly chose the cute alternative.

Each of the integrative approaches goes beyond a single-school limited focus and addresses more than one (and sometimes all) of the concerns highlighted by the mnemonic. There is also no suggestion of linear direction implied, and the circular model endorsed by the three-tier approach works here as well, as each of these concerns has impact on the others and reverberates throughout the treatment.

Figure 3.2

An Expanded Version of the Three-Tier Model

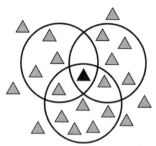

The mnemonic also forces attention to a clear shortcoming of the three-tier model as it has been promulgated. We have not paid any attention to biological or pharmacological processes and interventions, perhaps because we are focused on psychosocial rather than biological interventions, and perhaps because of the predominance of psychologists among the contributors to the psychotherapy integration movement. In any case, the integration of psychotherapy and pharmacotherapy is discussed nicely by Beitman and Saveanu (2005).

A more significant omission is the implication that the triangle in our three-tier model stands alone, rather than in the company of many other triangles. This is a particularly glaring omission in a model that fits within a relational framework. Clearly, the activity within each of the three tiers of any individual develops and is played out with relation to all the other significant individuals in the index person's world. Furthermore, all of the triangles exist in several cultural contexts, using culture in the broad sense defined by Cohen (2009), and that also requires our attention. Because individuals have more than one cultural context, a full description would include a Boolean set of circles that encompass these cultural contexts. A graphic representation of the expanded three-tier model is presented in Figure 3.2. The recognition of environment in the mnemonic serves as a necessary reminder that a more full description of the environment, taking into account both relationships and cultural contexts, must be added to augment the model. This omission will be corrected in future publications.

KEY CONCEPTS

The key concepts in psychotherapy integration have been summarized extensively and well in a textbook of that same name (Gold, 1996), and portions of this chapter will draw on that excellent work. In reviewing these key concepts, I will discuss them in terms of the therapeutic relationship and specific interventions.

The Therapeutic Relationship

The therapeutic relationship is a key concept in almost every approach to psychotherapy integration. It also is critical to almost every single school approach, making the relationship the foundation of almost any therapeutic approach. Just as the sale of real estate depends on location, location, location, the practice of psychotherapy depends on relationship, relationship, relationship. The therapeutic relationship can be described as an educational partnership, as the client comes to treatment to learn how to be different in ways determined by the therapeutic contract, and the therapist accepts the responsibility of teaching the client how to do that. It is important, in assuming this educational framework, to recognize that teaching does not imply any particular pedagogical stance, and there are Socratic as well as didactic or instructional approaches to this role.

One difficulty in integrating therapies lies in differences in these stances. If cognitive–behavioral therapists prefer a more instructional stance and psychodynamic therapists a more Socratic one, what will the therapist who integrates the two approaches be expected to do? Part of the skill in making integration seamless lies in moving from one stance to another without having a jarring effect on the relationship. The problem for the therapist has been made easier in recent years as cognitive–behavioral therapists have become more influenced by constructivist approaches and moved to a more inquiring and participatory stance (Safran, 1998), while psychodynamic therapists have become more willing to deal with behavior directly and moved to a greater willingness to suggest specific activities to their clients (Gold, 2005).

The therapeutic relationship, the working relationship, the transference–countertransference matrix, and the therapeutic alliance are terms that have been used almost interchangeably and refer to the relationship between the therapist and the client as they attempt to achieve the changes that the client has indicated are desirable. Bordin (1979) has described the necessary components of this alliance as consisting of the agreement on a goal, agreement on the means of reaching the goal, and establishing a bond that will facilitate the first two of these components. Although cognitive–behavioral therapists may focus more on interventions as a means of achieving the established goal, and psychodynamic therapists are more focused on the bond that exists, integrative therapists need to keep all of these components in mind as they establish a working relationship that will be productive. Perhaps the best distinction between the various approaches is that some therapists use the relationship as a foundation that the interventions rest on whereas others use it as a vehicle for change. Integrative therapists often place themselves at some point along this continuum, always valuing the relationship but using it differently. For assimilative psychodynamic integration, the relationship clearly is a vehicle, and much that is accomplished grows out of the client's experiences in the relationship.

Just as the role of the therapist differs from approach to approach, so does that of the client. In some approaches, the client is seen as a relatively passive absorber of information and direction, with activity directed to extratherapeutic endeavors in implementing the therapeutic instructions. In others, clients are active coparticipants, seeking to learn about themselves and to experience themselves in new and different ways. In some cases, the client becomes the director of the experience, determining the theory of the treatment and of change, directing appropriate activities and generally leading rather than following or joining in the therapeutic journey. Perhaps the best approach to understanding the variety of possible client roles (and, because they take a complementary role, that of therapists as well) is found in the work of Beutler (Beutler & Harwood, 2000; Beutler, Harwood, Bertoni, & Thomann, 2006), who describes various personality characteristics of clients that indicate whether a directive or passive approach is likely to be more successful. The reactant client, who does not take direction well, is better suited for a more indirect approach such as the psychodynamic, whereas clients low in reactance do well when the therapist is more directive, such as with cognitive–behavioral work. Beutler's approach to integration uses this and other distinctions to develop a treatment plan.

Alliance Ruptures

Because the treatment depends on a sound therapeutic alliance, it follows that the therapist is well advised to be alert to markers of alliance ruptures (disruptions in the therapeutic relationship) and to be prepared to take action to heal these ruptures as early as possible. Safran and Muran (1996) have written extensively about this and suggest the importance of a rapid and effective response to markers of ruptures in the therapeutic alliance. In addition to Safran and Muran, integrative therapists from many different approaches have made reference to alliance ruptures (Castonguay, Newman, Borkovec, Grosse Holtforth, & Maramba, 2005; Stricker & Gold, 2005; Weiss & Sampson, 1986; Wolfe, 2005). Because of the ubiquity of concern with the alliance and the central importance of detecting and healing ruptures, it is worth looking at this in greater depth.

Two types of alliance ruptures can be identified: withdrawal and confrontation (Safran, Muran, & Rothman, 2006). Withdrawal ruptures occur when the client disengages from the therapist, the therapeutic process, or his own emotions. Confrontation ruptures are marked by direct expressions of anger or dissatisfaction. In both types of ruptures, the indications can be direct and obvious, or more indirect and subtle. For example, a subtle withdrawal rupture might be indicated by a pseudoalliance, in which the client seems to be going through the motions of doing what is asked without actually engaging in the process of therapy. A subtle confrontation rupture may occur when the client refers to his dissatisfaction with an overbearing boss, who symbolically represents the therapist. When a rupture has been noted, through the appearance of a marker such as those mentioned, the therapist is best advised to respond to it quickly and to discuss it with the client. In doing so, it is most effective to empathize with the client's motivation to keep the alliance from developing and the characteristic nature of the client's response to closeness. However, it also is important not to blame the client for doing so and to recognize the contribution the therapist may be making to the lack of soundness in the alliance.

Enactment and Corrective Emotional Experience

This leads to the twin concepts of enactment and corrective emotional experience. An enactment occurs when the client repeats an earlier experience, in this case with the therapist, but also in many of the relationships in his life. For example, a client who was rejected by a parent in his childhood may enact this experience by finding relationships with rejecting figures and then may treat the therapist as though rejection is occurring in the therapeutic relationship. This is a clear signal of a potential rupture of the alliance, but it also is important information for the development of a change in the client's relationship style that will be salutary outside of the treatment situation. The therapist also must consider the extent to which she actually is being rejecting, as this also may contribute to the enactment and the rupture. The approach to healing this rupture and changing the dysfunctional pattern of relating is through the corrective emotional experience, by which the therapist refuses to participate in the enactment and to respond in a rejecting manner, but instead treats the client in a new and more positive manner. To the extent that this experience can be generalized outside of treatment, the client comes to realize that people are not necessarily rejecting, and it is possible to seek out relationships that are equally corrective rather than in persisting in seeking enactments of the earlier experience.

The consideration of enactments and the corrective emotional experience leads necessarily to thoughts of transference and countertransference:

> Transference as a process is present, in greater or lesser intensity, in all approaches to psychotherapy, whether or not the approach has a theoretical concept that recognizes the existence of the process. In fact, although transference technically refers to a relationship between a client and a therapist, something akin to transference occurs in many human relationships outside the therapeutic setting. Finally, transference, in this omnipresent sense, is the basis of a good deal of human dysfunction, and the ability to deal with it effectively underlies much that is reparative in psychotherapy. (Stricker, 2006c, p. 95)

An older concept of transference holds that it originates in the client (Greenson, 1967) and represents a projection onto the therapist of attitudes from earlier experiences. Greenson later recognized that there also is a working alliance that is not a product of distortion, and this concept is part of our concept of the therapeutic relationship. Aside from the projections and therapeutic alliance identified by Greenson, a real relationship exists between the client and the therapist. This real relationship cannot be dismissed as merely irrational transference and countertransference and is an inevitable part of the therapeutic relationship. Thus, a more current and relational approach to transference (Mitchell, 1988), which is embraced by assimilative psychodynamic integration, holds that transference is not a distortion based on projection but a creation of the client's, along with the therapist, of a manner of relating that also typifies other relationships the client has and has had. Viewed in this way, it closely resembles our views of an enactment.

Countertransference also has undergone significant changes over the history of psychodynamic thought. Initially, it was viewed as an imposition by the therapist into the pristine atmosphere of the therapeutic relationship and was to be avoided. More recently, and again within the relational model (Mitchell, 1988), it has come to mean the sum and substance of all of the feelings the therapist holds toward the client, and it is inevitable that such feelings arise in any human interaction. Thus, countertransference no longer is to be avoided and seen as a contaminant of treatment, but rather is a source of information about the relationship style of the client (and, at times, of the therapist). It is necessary for the therapist to be aware of the extent of countertransferential responses to avoid enactments and, by doing so, to be in a position to provide corrective emotional experiences.

As an example of this process, let us posit a client who has experienced rejection in his early experiences. He enters treatment with the expectation that he will be rejected, in therapy as in life, and sees rejection in even neutral comments by the therapist. The therapist, who prefers to see herself as nurturant and accepting, may respond to this perception of negativity by withdrawing, thereby engaging in an enactment and justifying the client's expectation of rejection. If the therapist is able to resist this temptation and instead persists in responding in an accepting and nurturing manner, a corrective emotional experience is provided, and the client may begin to reconsider his pervasive expectation of rejection.

Thus, we have seen how the psychotherapeutic relationship provides a microcosm of the style of relating of the client. The therapist who is alert to the attempts of the client to draw her into an enactment will resist these and instead will provide the corrective emotional experience that is a major curative aspect of psychotherapy.

Two aspects of this process must be emphasized at this point. First, the client is not a malevolent trickster attempting to tempt the therapist into an error based on the enactment. Rather, he is acting based on unconscious and habitual patterns and draws the therapist, as well as all other significant people in his life, into this dysfunctional pattern because it is the only style of relating that he knows. Relationships develop with others who are willing to play the part of accomplices (Wachtel, 1997) in this dysfunctional dance, and it is natural to expect the therapist to be among the many who are willing to do this. It is the therapist's ability to restrict this pull that leads to the corrective emotional experience and the opportunity to test out new patterns of relating outside the therapy room. However, the accomplices have a vested interest in the client remaining unchanged and will exert counterpressures. The skillful therapist will attempt to inoculate the client against these pressures by proper preparation. One advantage of the integrative approach is that the psychodynamic therapist is best at being aware of enactments and resisting them, but the cognitive–behavioral therapist is best at preparation for the world that awaits the changing client. The willingness to combine both approaches provides the best chance that the client has to develop new and more adaptive and satisfying relationship skills.

The second point to be emphasized in reviewing this pattern is that the language of enactments and corrective emotional experiences is the language of psychodynamic thought—more precisely relational psychodynamic thought—but the process being described occurs in all human relating. It is not necessary to adopt the jargon to appreciate the process. More and more, cognitive–behavioral therapists, particularly with a more constructivist viewpoint, are moving toward a willingness to recognize relational patterns and how they must be dealt with in order for behavioral changes to occur and be maintained. At the same time, psychodynamic therapists more and more are recognizing that simply understanding the pattern is not sufficient for meaningful change to occur, and more specific and targeted interventions are necessary for this change to occur. All of this fits well in a three-tier model, for the presence of behavioral, cognitive, and unconscious factors, and their necessary interrelatedness, are acknowledged, and the circularity and synergism of effect replaces a simple linear conception of change.

Client Participation

Some mention should also be made of another feature of the interpersonal relationship—the failure, unwillingness, or inability of the client to participate fully in the therapeutic process. Depending on the orientation of the therapist, this has been termed *resistance* (Greenson, 1967), *reactance* (Beutler et al., 2006), or *noncompliance* (Beck, Rush, Shaw, & Emery, 1979). In many cases, the onus has been placed on the client, and a resistant client is seen as a "bad" client. Any subsequent failure in treatment then can be attributed to shortcomings of the client rather than of the therapist. More recently this view of the phenomenon has shifted, with more attention being given to the therapist's role, or the interactive role, or the unconscious determinants, of this seeming barrier to treatment. Resistance then can be seen as the friend rather than the enemy of treatment, because it carries clues as to the client's typical means of functioning. For example, Beutler, Consoli, and Lane (2005) specifically plan the course of psychotherapy around the level of reactance of the client (among other factors), seeing more exploratory psychodynamic work as more in line with more reactant clients whereas clients low in reactance are more responsive to more directive cognitive–behavioral interventions. A demonstration to the client within the laboratory of the psychotherapy session of his unconscious and counterproductive difficulty in working meaningfully within the chosen and desired psychotherapeutic framework can be an effective way of highlighting this pattern of behavior. The therapist who can point this out gently and uncritically is setting the stage for a corrective emotional experience and avoiding the temptation to fall into an enactment of the typical and repetitive pattern that has been established. For example, the therapist previously mentioned, who is working with a client who anticipates rejection, might respond to withdrawal by wondering whether she might have done something to offend the client. This nonaccusatory intervention might help the client to recognize his contribution to the interaction and to begin a modification of that characteristic pattern. This new view of resistance also requires the therapist to be aware of ways that she may not be sufficiently responsive to the needs of the client, thus setting the groundwork for less productive work. Shared responsibility and understanding always seem to work better than blame, and the integrative therapist, not tied to any restricted framework, may be better suited to be aware of this problem and to transcend it.

The Role of the Relationship

After a careful review of the literature, Gold (1996) approached a consideration of the role of the relationship in psychotherapy integration by identifying three critical factors in the interaction. These are the emotional climate of the interaction, the interactional stance, and the role of interactional data. The first two of these are straightforward and can be easily defined:

> The emotional climate refers to the quality and quantity of affective engagement and involvement between client and therapist that are thought to be helpful, necessary, or ameliorative. Also important here are the specific types of affective and interpersonal experiences that are deemed to be positive, neutral, or destructive in the therapeutic work. (Gold, 1996, p. 90)

There is relatively widespread agreement about this. In assimilative psychodynamic integration, as in almost every other approach to psychotherapy integration, the emotional climate is seen as centrally important, and there is clear agreement that an empathic, accepting, and warm setting is best suited to therapeutic progress. In more pure form approaches, there may have been some initial disagreement, but recent changes have moved toward similar agreement as to the value of a warm emotional climate in therapy. Psychodynamic therapists, initially stereotyped as distant and unrevealing in the insight-oriented Freudian model, have become more embracing of the need for a warm emotional climate (Kohut, 1977).

Cognitive–behavioral therapists, although once primarily technique-oriented (Eysenck, 1960), also have moved to a position of more affective engagement (Goldfried & Davison, 1994). Humanistic approaches, of course, always prized the therapeutic relationship (Rogers, 1957). The major difference among the orientations, as also reflected in psychotherapy integration, depending on the strength of influence of the home theory, lies in the role of the relationship. Cognitive–behavioral approaches use the relationship as the foundation of subsequent treatment, psychodynamic approaches use the relationship as a vehicle for treatment, and humanistic approaches often see the relationship as both necessary and sufficient for therapeutic success. As Gold (1996) notes:

> The interactional stance in the therapeutic interaction is defined in terms of such issues as the therapist's activity level; the roles and responsibilities assigned to both client and therapist; and the place of the specific therapy on such continua as egalitarian versus authoritarian, directive versus nondirective, and exploratory versus didactic. (p. 92)

Again, the various approaches to psychotherapy integration are in some agreement, perhaps around a position best described as collaborative empiricism by Beck (Beck et al., 1979). The therapist is encouraged to be both didactic and exploratory, both directive and nondirective, depending on the therapeutic circumstances. There is little value placed on authoritarianism, and to the extent that the therapist is acting in a didactic or directive way, it is in a collaborative fashion after enlisting the client's agreement.

Thus, for both emotional climate and interactional stance, there is agreement among the various approaches to psychotherapy integration as to the best position for the therapist to assume. There also is little disagreement with the more contemporary versions of most of the single school approaches, as they also advocate a flexible stance suited to the individual client within a warm interpersonal climate. There is more variability in terms of the orientation toward interactional data assumed by the various approaches. Gold identified three different modes, "the *intrapsychic–transferential mode,* the *interpersonal–characterological mode,* and the *prizing–safety mode*" (Gold, 1996, p. 96, italics in original).

The intrapsychic–transferential mode focuses on the unconscious determinants that help to shape the current interpersonal relationship between the client and the therapist. This suggests that there is some weight placed on the possible distortion of the client's view of the therapist by past experiences, and the therapist's possible contributions to the interaction is given less weight. This emphasis on unconsciously determined transference reactions places the approach clearly in line with more classical approaches to psychoanalytic thinking and appears prominently in integrative approaches that draw upon this source, as least in part. One example of this approach (Papouchis & Passman, 1993) is an attempt to apply traditional psychodynamic concepts along with other techniques to psychotherapy with the elderly. An important implication of the intrapsychic–transferential mode is the use of interpretations that promote insight as a prime technique.

The interpersonal–characterological mode is more cognizant of the joint contributions of the client and the therapist to the interaction and sees the present as important without discounting the influence of the past. Thus, a good part of the response of the client can be understood in light of the contributions of the therapist to the interaction, although the possibility exists that this contribution can be shaped by, and understood in light of, the client's past experiences. Clearly, this owes a debt to more contemporary interpersonal approaches to psychodynamic thinking, but it also is present in more contemporary cognitive–behavioral thought as well. Wachtel (1977) introduced this mode of thought to the integrative literature, and it is echoed in many psychodynamic (Stricker, 2006a) and cognitive–behavioral (Castonguay et al., 2005) writings. This leads to interventions that avoid enactments and create corrective emotional experiences for the client.

The prizing–safety mode emphasizes that aspect of the therapeutic relationship that can be called the real relationship (Greenson, 1967), the relationship that emerges out of the interaction of two human beings without regard to distortions created or shaped by past experiences. This grows out of a humanistic approach to psychotherapy and is exemplified in the work of authors who are most influenced by this approach (e.g., Watson, 2006). Affirming interventions such as prizing are prominent and are seen as valuable in leading to a collaborative alliance that allows the work of psychotherapy to be accomplished.

Previously, I have noted that the boundaries between the types of psychotherapy integration are fluid, and it is easier to describe different approaches than it is to classify approaches to psychotherapy integration. There is much overlap in some of the approaches that have been presented, so that, for example, whether the work of Lazarus (2005) can be considered technical integration or assimilative integration is neither clear nor particularly important. Similarly, the modes of approach to interactional data can be described clearly, but classifying individual approaches muddies the waters somewhat. As an easy example, our own work, assimilative psychodynamic integration (Gold & Stricker, 2001; Stricker & Gold, 2002; Stricker, 2006a), relies primarily on the interpersonal–characterological mode but also incorporates some of the thinking from the more traditional intrapsychic–transferential mode and some of the interventions of the prizing–safety mode. Classification, often within arbitrary categories, rarely carves nature at its joints and more usually is only valuable in pointing to general differences rather than specific instances of each type.

Specific Interventions

Specific interventions refer to everything the psychotherapist does. It is important to note that this includes both dramatic actions such as the suggestion of activities to the client as well as more subtle activities such as listening carefully or choosing not to respond. A psychotherapy session is filled with choice points, and at each one the therapist intervenes, either by doing something or by choosing not to do anything at that time. It is this broad conception of an intervention that gives the lie to the traditional notion of the psychotherapist remaining silent in order to allow the client to use the therapist as a screen and project unconscious wishes and fantasies into the interaction. Although such projection may occur and should be noted, the silent therapist can easily be seen as aloof or rejecting, and this is not a distortion but a response to a real response in the immediate interaction.

In approaching the topic of interventions, I will use the acronym ABCDEF that was cited previously. Each of the areas of entry identified

Table 3.1

The ABCDEF Mnemonic

	Meaning	Therapeutic Approach	Sample Interventions
A	Affect	Humanistic therapy	Prizing, chair work
B	Behavior	Behavior therapy	Skills training, directive instructions
C	Cognition	Cognitive therapy	Challenging, homework
D	Dynamics	Psychodynamic therapy	Clarification, confrontation, interpretation
E	Environment	Systems theory	Couples therapy, family therapy
F	Fysiology	Psychopharmacology	Medication

by the acronym can serve as the primary focus of an intervention, and the integrative therapist has the advantage of being able to draw upon all of them rather than being restricted to the few that fall within the purview of a particular theoretical orientation. A summary of this approach is presented in Table 3.1.

Affect

Interventions that address affect typically originate in the humanistic school of treatment. It is important to distinguish between in-session interventions that are intended to alter the experience of affect in the immediate session and treatment plans that address changes in overall affect states. As to the latter, there are well-developed protocols for the resolution of depression (Beck et al., 1979) or anxiety (Wolfe, 2005). Those are not the focus of this section. I also will not spend a great deal of time addressing attempts to alter the in-session experience, such as anxiety reduction, which is well treated by approaches derived from the behavioral tradition, such as systematic desensitization (Wolpe & Lazarus, 1966). Instead, the focus will be on techniques that increase emotional awareness and experiencing during the therapy session.

Two different approaches to heightening affective experiences can be discerned. The first involves creating a therapeutic climate in which the client feels free and safe enough to experience fully and disclose his entire range of affective experience. These strategies typically involve prizing the client and providing the full range of Rogers's necessary and sufficient conditions for therapeutic change (Rogers, 1957). Although these strategies originated with Rogers and have become central to therapy in his tradition, they are also widely adopted in many other single school approaches and almost every integrative approach. These strategies were discussed previously under the rubric of the therapeutic relationship.

The second approach involves the direct use of an intervention, or therapeutic exercise, to heighten affective experience and authenticity. One excellent example of such exercises is referred to as *chair work* (Rice & Greenberg, 1992). The two common variants are known as the empty-chair and the two-chair techniques. In the empty-chair technique, the client is asked to address an empty chair in which a significant person in his life is imagined to sit. This allows the possibility of an imaginal dialogue with an important person and can lead to the expression of feelings that have been difficult to access. In the two-chair technique, the client imagines that one part of him is in one chair and another part in the other chair; the client moves from chair to chair as the two parts have a discussion with each other. Thus, for example, the adventurous and the timid parts of a person might have a dialogue, with the encouragement and occasional participation of the therapist, and conflicts around activity can be accessed. Chair work is readily adopted in many integrative approaches that originate in foundations other than the humanistic (Goldfried & Davison, 1994; Stricker, 2006a) and serves the purpose of increasing affective experience that then can be worked with within the home theory of the therapist.

It also should be noted that an essentially psychodynamic integrative approach, accelerated experiential dynamic psychotherapy (Fosha, 2002), also emphasizes emotional arousal and relatedness in psychotherapy. This approach combines the prizing relational attitudes with some active interventions that heighten emotional experience and does so in order to encourage the characterological transformation that is associated with psychodynamic psychotherapy.

Behavior

Interventions that address behavior typically originate in the behavioral school of treatment. These interventions address behavior directly; although any intervention can be considered to address behavior indirectly and at the end of a long chain of changes. These interventions have direct impact on behavior as well as a possible indirect impact on other dimensions of function and, as such, may be incorporated within psychodynamic approaches. Behavior therapy stimulates change, whether it is in the learning of adaptive capacities, the correction of cognitive distortions, or the experience of the self in new ways (Goldfried, 1991). Of course, Goldfried, who presented this formulation, is one of the key figures in psychotherapy integration, and so we would expect him to have a broad vision. The use of change in self-experience has already been discussed, and the use of change for cognitive distortions will be addressed subsequently. Let us now look at the learning of skills.

One approach to the learning of skills is instruction in specific areas of problem solving. This is particularly popular when working with children (Foster & Crain, 2002) and includes areas such as learning social skills and dealing more effectively with problematic situations. With adults, it often takes the form of learning specific skills, such as in relaxation training, assertion training, and behavioral rehearsal (Goldfried & Davison, 1994). Each of these techniques can be incorporated within an integrative approach to treatment, supplementing whatever other interventions and approaches are being used.

An additional approach to changing behavior is for the therapist to adopt a directive approach, a stance that is easily incorporated within a more traditional behavioral psychotherapy, but one that is foreign to more psychodynamic or humanistic approaches to treatment. However, Freud, who we already have noted as a potential candidate for the first integrative therapist, did recommend that the treatment of some obsessive and phobic clients required direct exposure to the phobic object (Freud, 1912/1961) or exhortation to discontinue ritualistic behavior (Freud, 1909/1961). In addition, Alexander and French (1946) raised the question as to whether insight and behavior change might have a bidirectional influence, so that behavior change might, on occasion, lead to insight, rather than an exclusive linear influence from insight to behavior change. This represents the type of accommodation that is necessary in any integrative approach, particularly one based on assimilation. In addition, we already have noted how specific directive humanistic interventions, such as chair work, are used in heightening affective experience and self-knowledge (Rice & Greenberg, 1992). Finally, a directive approach is also incorporated in dialectical behavior therapy (Heard & Linehan, 2005), which is more rooted in a behavioral approach but goes well beyond that pure form approach to the treatment of borderline personality disorder.

Gold (1996) distinguishes between two integrative approaches to these action-oriented techniques. The first of these is prescriptive and the second is aimed at creating psychodynamic as well as behavioral change. The prescriptive approaches attempt to match the treatment technique with specific client characteristics. The most elaborate system of prescriptive matching has been accomplished by Beutler and colleagues (2005) and involves, as has been described, a choice of techniques dependent on client characteristics. Another system, this time based more on symptom presentation than more characterological dimensions, has been developed by Lazarus (2005) and uses the BASIC-ID that also has been described previously.

Gold (1996) further distinguishes between two subgroups of the more psychodynamic approach to action-oriented techniques. These correspond to the one-person and two-person psychodynamic approaches, or the more intrapsychic and interpersonal approaches. It is important to remember that these approaches, although psychodynamic, are directed to behavior change as well as to more dynamic issues. Within the intrapsychic category are a variety of approaches that attempt to uncover conflicts through the direct activation of behavioral issues. The most comprehensive such system that I have described previously is that of Wolfe (2005), who uses active interventions to gain insight into the self-wounds that underlie many anxiety disorders. Gold's work (1993) also uses in vivo techniques to reduce anxiety symptoms as well as to gain greater insight into underlying conflicts, building on much historically important work in doing so (e.g., Feather & Rhodes, 1972).

The more contextual, relational approaches are based on the conception that behavior patterns are part of a cyclical pattern in which people's actions elicit and are maintained by the responses of others with whom they interact. Foremost among these approaches is that of Wachtel (1997), although several more constructivist and cognitive approaches (Safran et al., 2006) also adopt this stance. The key concept here is Wachtel's idea of the accomplice (for Safran, it involves hooking others into a relationship), the person who plays a complementary, enabling role in a dysfunctional relationship. By directly interceding in that relationship, behavioral changes can be accomplished and recognition of the pattern and its basis can also be achieved. Ryle's approach (Ryle & Low, 1993) also relies on this recognition of the reliance on others for the maintenance of dysfunctional relationships and the need for both insight and direct intercession to heal these patterns.

Cognition

Interventions that address cognition typically originate in the cognitive school of treatment. Cognitive approaches share many of the characteristics of the behavioral approaches that have just been described. They are active interventions, although they target patterns of thought rather than action. They have direct impact on thought as well as impact on other dimensions of function and, as such, are readily incorporated within psychodynamic approaches. Of course, the most influential integrative approach to treatment is cognitive–behavioral therapy (Beck et al., 1979), which targets the two foci of behavior and cognition.

The combination of the psychodynamic and the cognitive approach probably is the most frequently noted of all of the integrative efforts. Some of these originate in the psychodynamic school (e.g., Ryle & Low, 1993), whereas others seem to begin with a more cognitive perspective (e.g., Safran, 1998). This is an easy path because psychodynamic thinking does have a heavy cognitive component, given its emphasis on insight, and cognitive thinking often seeks out the origin of dysfunctional thought patterns, using concepts such as the schema (Young, 1999). Regardless of the point of origin, the two converging notions are that certain patterns of thought originate early and become ingrained, and these, in turn, affect behavior. Whether the change then leads to efforts to alter the dysfunctional thought pattern or to first understand the origin is a matter of dispute, but the cyclical nature of many integrative formulations holds that the point of entry into the system does not matter, and either one will reverberate and have an impact on the other. Thus, the integrative viewpoint easily can accommodate both approaches without being preoccupied with the chicken-and-egg question of initial point of entry.

Among the cognitive interventions that are prominent are such tactics as challenging dysfunctional (irrational) patterns of thought, an approach that originated in rational emotive therapy (Ellis, 1962). Although Ellis had little use for psychodynamic approaches, his way of working is similar to the confrontation that marks much recent interpersonal psychodynamic efforts. The use of homework assignments also originated in cognitive and behavioral treatments but can be adopted easily into more psychodynamic work (Stricker, 2007). The three points of intervention that have been noted— affect, behavior, and cognition—are not easily disentangled: Interventions placed in one category might fit well in another, and the combination of the three is often seen. That this is true provides support for working integratively and not seeking an artificial separation among these points of intervention. In each of these cases, integration with a psychodynamic approach follows naturally, and we will next turn to that approach.

Dynamics

Interventions that address dynamics typically originate in the psychodynamic school of treatment. Ordinarily, we do not think of many interventions associated with psychodynamic therapy, as the major approach is listening and understanding. However, listening often is followed by interpretation, an intervention designed to give previously unappreciated meaning to a pattern of behavior. Recently, other active interpretations, such as confrontation and clarification, have become prominent in the repertoire of psychodynamic therapists (Weiner & Bornstein, 2009). Confrontation refers to such interventions as directly indicating the existence of a particular dysfunctional behavior to a client or asking him about discrepancies between contradictory statements or actions. Clarification consists of an exploration of the meaning of a pattern of events or behaviors. In addition to these strategies, there also are particular activities that are more likely to be practiced by psychodynamic therapists, such as the report and interpretation of dreams or early memories, and the exploration of possible antecedent events with an eye toward furthering understanding.

It is interesting to note that each of the specific strategies—interpretation, confrontation, and clarification—have a parallel strategy that is practiced by cognitive therapists. The difference between a characterological pattern and a cognitive schema may lie in the language preference of the therapist, and so the means to approach dealing with this pattern should have similarities to each other. In both cases, a consistent and dysfunctional pattern is approached by an attempt to increase understanding and then to translate that understanding into behavior change. Integration is not difficult when the underlying activities to be integrated are not as different as language would lead us to believe. Among the many integrative approaches that combine psychodynamic and cognitive–behavioral approaches on a theoretical level are those of Wachtel (1977), Ryle (Ryle & Low, 1993), and Castonguay (Castonguay et al., 2005).

Integration of the psychodynamic and the humanistic approaches might be less obvious but perhaps are more easily done. The humanistic approach tends not to value the impact of the past as highly as do psychodynamic theorists, but it does look to understanding as a vehicle for change. One example of this approach that seems to incorporate some of these psychodynamic strategies was presented by Bugenthal (Bugenthal & Kleiner, 1993).

Although there are some great similarities between the interventions adopted by psychodynamic, cognitive, and humanistic theorists, the differences among these approaches are more than simply linguistic. It is the role of the unconscious that most clearly separates the theories. Cognitive theorists often acknowledge the existence of processes that are not within the immediate awareness of the client, and this does appear to be similar to an unconscious, but it is the presence of an active, dynamic unconscious that marks the psychodynamic approach as distinct from the other two. Nonetheless, in terms of interventions, a clear similarity can be seen among each of them. Thus, the therapist may ask the client about discrepancies between contradictory statements or actions in any of these approaches, conceptualizing and naming it differently but doing the same thing.

Environment

Interventions that address the environment typically originate in the systems schools of treatment. One can view systems on many levels. Some systems exist within an individual, as demonstrated most graphically by the three-tier model (Gold & Stricker, 1993; Stricker & Gold, 1988). Other systems exist between individuals, as exemplified by the various family therapy approaches to psychotherapy. Still others, within which individuals and families exist, are the cultural conditions that are crucial for our understanding yet that often are neglected in approaching psychotherapy. Each of these systems has been addressed by different approaches to psychotherapy integration.

One of the best developed of these systems approaches is integrative problem-centered therapy (Pinsof, 2005), an approach that has an extensive description of the relevant systems that have an impact on an individual, including each of those outlined previously. Depending on the nature of the problem, intervention may occur at the individual, family, or environmental level and may be drawn from any of a number of approaches to psychotherapy. The presenting problem is ranked from the broadest point of intervention, the organizational, to the most individual, the self system. Similarly, the orientations are ranked in complexity from the behavioral through self-psychology. The contexts for intervention are the family/community, the couple, and the individual. These rankings are then organized in a matrix so that the first attempt at intervention would be a behavioral approach within the breadth of the family; if this is not successful, successive interventions would be attempted until self-psychology would be used with the individual. This notion of coexisting systems with different targets depending on the problem being treated is integrative in nature and unusually thorough in implementation.

The first major approach to assume the intraindividual systems stance, recognizing that changes in one aspect of the person's functioning reverberate and lead to other, often synergistic, changes, was cyclical psychodynamics (Wachtel, 1977). As a watershed work, it provided an important precedent for many works that followed and adopted the same approach to change. Of course, in a less developed way, Alexander and French (1946) already had suggested the bidirectional nature of the relationship between insight and change. Our own work, the three-tier model (Gold & Stricker, 1993; Stricker & Gold, 1988), already has been described and discusses the reciprocal relationships among behavior, cognition, affect, and psychodynamic processes.

The most well-developed systems approaches are interindividual and are in the area of family therapy. Many approaches to family therapy clearly are integrative in nature (e.g., Lebow, 2006). Here, too, similar to Pinsof (2005), there is a clear and explicit recognition that problems exist at many levels and at various levels within the social system. Thus, couple therapy, a clearly systemic approach, takes into account that the couple is part of a larger social system and also consists of two individuals, each of whom has his or her own internal system. Interventions are chosen to respond to each of these active levels, with the choice depending on the target problem that has been agreed upon by the therapist and client (another example of client-driven therapy). It also is noteworthy that Lebow (2006) notes that his practice is "strongly informed by the relevant science yet takes into account what I can do best" (p. 213). The matter of evidence-based practice is a critical one and will be discussed in a later chapter. The recognition that each therapist has preferences, strengths, and limitations should go without saying, and all too often it does go without saying. Nonetheless, it is important to say, and to acknowledge that each therapist should only work in areas of personal as well as professional competence.

Unified therapy (Allen, 2006) has a somewhat different approach to the interindividual systems approach. It essentially pursues an integrated approach to individual therapy, but with the recognition that any change occurring in the therapy office will have an impact on the client's family system, which may serve to move toward a restoration of equilibrium at the expense of any changes that have been achieved in treatment. Thus, the therapist makes a conscious attempt to take this into account and to anticipate this pressure for a restoration of the preexisting system by preparing the client to deal with it. The preparation sometimes goes as far as to suggest ways in which the client can approach family members and to role-play these anticipated meetings. Thus, a systems approach is being used within an individual therapy format, and interventions from cognitive, psychodynamic, and humanistic approaches are integrated with this systems perspective.

Fysiology

Interventions that address physiology typically originate in the psychopharmacological approach to treatment. Although it is reasonable to expect that many therapy clients will present with issues amenable to medication, it is unusual for descriptions of psychosocial treatment to include this possibility. Some integrative approaches explicitly consider the possibility of pharmacological intervention (Lazarus, 2005; Wolfe, 2005), but even these approaches usually describe cases that do not have a pharmacological dimension. The alternative is for the integration of pharmacology and psychotherapy to be considered as an integrative approach in its own right (Beitman & Saveanu, 2005), but the specific nature of psychotherapy is not a focus on this consideration of combined therapy. Interestingly, in Beitman's work specifically on psychotherapy (Beitman & Yue, 1999), little attention is given to pharmacology. It appears that this area is still in need of much attention, as some approaches to psychotherapy might be preferable to others when combined with medication, and no sophisticated consideration of this matter has been developed within the integrative literature.

The larger dimension of the biological is not limited to pharmacological treatment. Physical dimensions to psychological problems require consideration, and there always is a need to determine that problems are indeed psychological rather than solely physical in origin (even physical problems have a psychological dimension and can be treated, but it is a different matter to treat the sequelae rather than the causes of a problem). This is particularly obvious with many of the anxiety disorders, which have clear physical manifestations and may require medical as well as psychological interventions. Wolfe (2005) is particularly clear about taking this into consideration.

INTEGRATION AND DIVERSITY

Diversity is a concept that embraces many dimensions. Among these, the Ethics Code lists "age, gender, gender identity, race, ethnicity, culture, national origin, religion, sexual orientation, disability, language, and socioeconomic status" (American Psychological Association, 2002, p. 63). Psychotherapy in general, as well as psychotherapy integration in particular, has not addressed diversity in all of its complexity. As far as evidence is concerned, the majority of randomized control trials have been conducted with a carefully selected client population and generalization to a diverse clientele is not clearly established. However, psychotherapy integration, because of its flexibility and willingness to adapt to different circumstances, shows promise in being able to adjust to the needs of a variety of people. With the recognition that many areas are not directly addressed, we shall look at areas where integrative approaches have been developed.

Areas such as national origin and culture are well addressed by workers in psychotherapy integration. Wachtel (2008) summarized a symposium featuring an international perspective on psychotherapy integration. At this symposium, the state of psychotherapy integration around the world was discussed, and these contributions were summarized in a series of articles in the *Journal of Psychotherapy Integration*. This special section of the journal summarized the state of psychotherapy integration, not only in the United States (Hartston, 2008), but also in Portugal (Vasco, 2008), in Switzerland and Germany (Caspar, 2008), in Argentina (Fernandez-Alvarez, 2008), in Chile (Opazo & Bagladi, 2008), and in Japan (Iwakabe, 2008). The cultural differences expressed, as well as some of the similarities across countries, were stimulating at the symposium and remain stimulating in their written expression.

In this same vein, a recent collection of contributions to psychotherapy integration was published by European editors (O'Leary & Murphy, 2006), and it has no overlap at all with the handbook published in North America at the same time (Norcross & Goldfried, 2005a). The striking difference between the two collections is in the emphasis, in the United

States, on psychodynamic and cognitive–behavioral approaches, and in Ireland, on humanistic approaches. One wonders about what an Asian collection would look like and also marvels at the wide scope and variety of integrative efforts.

As to gender, an important source of diversity, feminist therapy (e.g., Enns, 2004), is necessarily an integrative approach. It focuses on cultural and relationship issues, seeking to empower women by stressing equality and drawing on many different approaches to accomplish these goals. Feminist therapy also integrates a concern for multiculturalism and a recognition of sexual orientation as an additional source of diversity requiring attention.

Moving to sexual orientation, one of the pivotal figures in psychotherapy integration, Marvin Goldfried, recently has turned his attention to this area and developed an organization, AFFIRM: Psychologists Affirming their Lesbian, Gay, Bisexual, and Transgender Family (http://naples.cc.sunysb.edu/CAS/affirm.nsf), that encourages sensitivity to the role of sexual orientation in all clinical and research work. He has published on considerations in the treatment of gay, lesbian, and bisexual clients (Eubanks-Carter, Burckell, & Goldfried, 2005a; Pachankis & Goldfried, 2004), and these publications, as would be expected, are heavily informed by psychotherapy integration.

Age appears to be an important diversity issue, but psychotherapy integration has been concerned primarily with adult psychotherapy. Both children and older adults require flexibility and variety in therapeutic approach, and most writing has emphasized that point but has not been identified with psychotherapy integration. Exceptions exist for children (Coonerty, 1993; Keat, 1990) and older adults (Papouchis & Passman, 1993), but unfortunately these are rare. Similarly, religion, disability, and socioeconomic status are not often addressed as diversity issues within psychotherapy integration. There are some exceptions with disability (Becker, 1993; Dworkin & Grzesiak, 1993), and spirituality has often been seen as a variable to be integrated in treatment (Sollod, 2005), but more generally, these dimensions of diversity have not been stressed.

Race and ethnicity have been addressed directly, as has been noted previously, both in general terms (Ivey & Brooks-Harris, 2005) and in relationship to African Americans (Franklin, Carter, & Grace, 1993). These works recognize the importance of cultural variables in constructing an integrated treatment plan and are important contributions to our ability to deal with the complexity of ethnicity as part of the fabric of human personality.

We have seen the many manifestations of issues that the client may bring to treatment, diversity considerations about the client, and the manifold responses available to the integrative therapist. It now is time to turn to some specific applications of these processes.

4

The Therapy Process

Although I could have used all of my own cases to illustrate change mechanisms, I would prefer to do justice to the full range of psychotherapy integration. For that reason, I will be summarizing several case studies that other contributors have published. However, in each case, I will compare the approach to assimilative psychodynamic integration to clarify the similarities and differences.

CASE EXAMPLES

Common Factors

Among the many contributors in this area, Beitman (Beitman, Soth, & Bumby, 2005; Beitman, Soth, & Good, 2006) and his emphasis on the future as the integrating common factor is one of the most influential. In this approach, Beitman views the client as a teleological creature and sees all theories as united by their emphasis on the client's future. His concept of the expectation video, or mental movie of one's future, is critical to each client, and the alteration of past expectation videos, along with the co-construction of newer and healthier ones, is the key process in his approach to psychotherapy integration. The specific intervention includes a four-step model that consists of (1) identification of problematic responses; (2) identifying mismatches between expectations and experiences; (3) specification of the expectation video that was based on the mismatch; and (4) alteration of either the expectations or the experiences so that the mismatch is resolved. The impetus for this approach was the case of Kathy (Beitman et al., 2006), which is summarized here.

> "Kathy, a 22-year-old, European American, heterosexual, middle-class woman, presented with reports of panic attacks and depressed mood of 6 years' duration. She also reported a history of difficult interpersonal relationships. Kathy had grown up in a small midwestern town that she described as a sheltering, conservative, and community-oriented environment. She reported that she had one older brother and that she had a mother who dominated her father. When Kathy was 5 years old, her father had an affair, divorced her mother, and remarried, often leaving Kathy under the care of a new stepmother. This woman, 'the bitch my father sleeps with,' physically and emotionally abused Kathy throughout her developmental years. Kathy reported that her father consistently sided with his new wife's criticism of Kathy and that her birth mother was only superficially supportive. Kathy's closest childhood friend, through whom she escaped the pressures of home, died after falling off of a rooftop when he was 13. When Kathy was 17, preparing for a dance recital, her best male friend was rushed to the hospital where he died of a rare virus. At age 20, Kathy's brother died suddenly while wrestling with his roommates. She described her romantic relationships as nongratifying, imbalanced, and short-lived. Kathy was a senior theater major at a large midwestern university when she came into psychotherapy" (p. 49). Kathy was taking Prozac at the time therapy began, and her diagnosis was recurrent major depression and panic disorder without agoraphobia.

The theme of loss was identified as a crucial one, and Kathy was given a homework assignment to prepare a timeline of her loss experiences. She recognized that the losses were all of important males and that she was not present at the deaths of any of them. She then engaged in an empty-chair exercise, speaking to, and apologizing to, each of the deceased people for whom she was grieving. However unlikely, Kathy felt as though she were responsible for their deaths by jinxing them and so apologized for her presumed role in their deaths.

Her roommate Jenna was noisy and was not contributing her share of the expenses of the apartment they shared. Kathy recognized that her inability to confront this situation was related to her fear that an aggressive action might lead to Jenna leaving, and perhaps even dying, as so many other significant people had done. In addition, Kathy also reported that her romantic relationships always were short-lived, even though she said she wanted to form a lasting relationship, because she became fearful of a loss and prematurely terminated the relationship.

Having identified Kathy's problematic relationships, it was a short step to develop appropriate expectation videos. Kathy had expectations that involved some combination of the loss of a significant person, betrayal and abandonment in close relationships, lost identity if she pursued intimacy, and the fear of eventual loneliness. She was encouraged to test these expectations against her experiences, which contained some contradictory evidence and much that could be interpreted in ways other than what was seen in Kathy's expectation videos. The contrast between Kathy's early experiences and her current experiences, which were shaped and colored by the earlier experiences, led her to begin to construct new expectations for future experiences. As she did so, she felt more calm and in control, and developed a healthy relationship with a man.

In reviewing this case, it is clear how Beitman's focus on the future led to a rearrangement of Kathy's priorities and led to significant changes in her pattern of relationships. The emphasis on the future as the common factor is the basis of the approach. Technical integration also is present as techniques from several approaches are integrated (empty-chair work, homework, cognitive restructuring of her experiences, and interpretation of the impact of past events).

In comparison to assimilative psychodynamic integration, this case does not have a central theoretical focus, emphasizing the future rather than relational psychotherapy as the coordinating concept. However, it does display the wide range of interventions that might be seen in assimilative psychodynamic integration.

Technical Integration

Although Lazarus was the first person to present a complete system, the case summarized here was contributed by Beutler (Beutler, Harwood, Bertoni, & Thomann, 2006) and is representative of prescriptive psychotherapy.

> "Frank was a 39-year-old Caucasian male with 14 years of education who had been married for about 3 years and had no children. He had just started a home-based business with his wife, after having held several jobs in the past few years. He decided to see a psychologist because he was experiencing severe financial problems caused by his drug abuse (he was in debt to pay for his drugs), and his wife was threatening to leave him if he did not find a definitive solution to his addiction. He also reported symptoms of anxiety, sometimes feeling 'overwhelmed by a lack of motivation,' and talked about having 'no desire to do anything,' all of which are characteristics of severe depression. He was 'tired of lying to himself and to others.'" (p. 31).

Frank arrived late for the first session and was given a standard battery of psychological tests to evaluate him on the dimensions critical to prescriptive psychotherapy. Frank was attending both Alcoholics Anonymous and Narcotics Anonymous, but also was actively using both heroin and cocaine. His parents divorced when he was 14 and his father then disappeared. His mother, who abused him, later committed suicide. He drank heavily as a teenager, began using heroin as an adult, and, shortly before therapy began, when reminded of the abuse he had experienced, made a suicide attempt.

Frank had a history of beginning treatment with a high level of anxiety, but this quickly dissipated and his motivation decreased along with it. Initially, much support was provided to build the therapeutic alliance and keep Frank committed to the treatment. However, treatment also required the maintenance of a sufficient level of anxiety to keep Frank motivated and in treatment and, as a result, some confrontation was included. Although an increase of anxiety sounds countertherapeutic, without some anxiety there is no perception of need and it is difficult to keep clients in treatment. Interventions alternated, with support provided when Frank was distressed and confrontation used when he became more complacent.

With therapy designed in this manner, treatment began by targeting drug abuse with educational efforts, homework, and some insight-seeking activities. Within 20 sessions, Frank was attending Narcotics Anonymous sessions and participating in a methadone program. When he stopped using drugs, he began to establish contacts outside the drug-using community, started a new job, and seemed able to resurrect his marriage and financial situation. At this point he was able to face some of the earlier problems that had plagued him and began to look at the impact of his childhood on his present functioning.

Frank's treatment shows the key features of prescriptive therapy. He was assessed on a series of relevant dimensions, on the basis of which a series of treatment decisions was made. Frank's level of impairment was considered moderate, based on his drug abuse and suicide attempt. His social support was weak and the numerous areas of functioning it affected supported the description of his problem as complex. This led to a decision about the intensity of treatment required. Although his drug use and suicidal behavior were of great concern, hospitalization was not required. Instead, Frank was assigned to be seen twice weekly initially, with a subsequent reduction as his improvement dictated, but with an expectation for long-term treatment. A plan for reduction of drug use was developed, supplemented by much educational material and a monitoring of attendance at Alcoholics Anonymous and Narcotics Anonymous meetings.

In terms of coping style, Frank had both externalizing (substance abuse) and internalizing (suicidality) features. The initial target was the externalizing behavior, specifically in terms of developing impulse control, but the long-term development of insight, in response to his internalizing, also was planned. Frank's level of resistance was low average, suggesting that he would respond to directiveness on the part of the therapist. Therefore, appropriate homework assignments were given. When the therapist sensed an increase in resistance, the level of directiveness was reduced. The treatment itself used interventions drawn from a broad range of theories, without regard to the theoretical basis for those interventions, as is characteristic of technical integration.

Technical integration uses a much more elaborate set of initial assessment devices than assimilative psychodynamic integration. The results of this assessment, rather than a central theoretical approach, unify the treatment that follows. However, the multiple styles of interventions are consistent with assimilative psychodynamic integration, and with every other approach to psychotherapy integration.

Theoretical Integration

Wachtel's (1977) seminal book integrated psychodynamic thought, primarily of a relational nature, with the behavioral approach. The system that was presented, cyclical psychodynamics, inspired much that followed and is a landmark work in this area. One case that exemplifies the approach is that of John (Wachtel, Kruk, & McKinney, 2005).

> John, a middle-aged Caucasian man, was a prominent psychologist who had been unable to pass the licensing exam, having failed five times, despite his central role in the field. His presenting concern, test anxiety, came in the context of a family background that valued excellence rather than mere competence. He was not comfortable as a client and preferred emphasizing his professional and social position. This highlighted the concern his parents had about status, and John was provided with some relief when he was able to confess these status concerns. Consciously, John was less concerned with status, and so attributing the origin of those concerns to his parents allowed him to acknowledge and deal with them. This gentle confrontation about John's status concerns led to a recognition that he was insulted by having to take the exam, did not take it seriously, and as a result did not prepare properly for it. His casual approach to the exam undermined the likelihood of passing and added to his anxiety each time he failed.

The therapeutic approach to the anxiety was twofold. First, the dynamics that led to John's dismissive attitude and self-destructive failure to prepare properly for the exam was explored and helped John to prepare in a more satisfactory manner. At the same time, the anxiety was addressed directly through interventions such as systematic desensitization. The sequence was to provide some insight first, to follow this with the anxiety-reducing exercises, and then to have more insight-oriented work. The images connected with desensitization heightened John's awareness of his indignation at being considered part of the crowd taking the exam. Each new image that was used in the desensitization led to a series of associations that uncovered further feelings of being demeaned and feeling weak and inadequate. As John became aware of this, he was able to deal with it more adequately and to prepare for the exam in a more appropriate and anxiety-free manner.

Perhaps the most interesting set of associations came to a wave of anxiety that John experienced and later associated with an image of a panther behind him. This was related to his fear of his own power and aggression and led to an incorporation of the panther within himself. The panther also was portrayed as a graceful, powerful, but respectful predator who never underestimated his prey. The panther image was helpful in this instance and also in other issues that John dealt with in the treatment. John passed the exam and did so with little difficulty and some distinction, in keeping with the ability he always had but never used for this task.

The cyclical nature of this treatment is apparent. The insight initially achieved led to and shaped the incorporation of behavioral interventions, which produced behavior change and, in turn, led to further insight. Although the focus was more specific than is usually the case in this approach, the ramifications were broad. John not only was able to pass the exam, his initial goal, but also was able to achieve considerable self-understanding concerning pressures from his parents that promoted other changes in his functioning. The combination of exploration of internal experiences with direct interventions to promote behavior change is the hallmark of this approach and of much that follows in psychotherapy integration.

Two other points are worth noting. First, the issue of status was approached indirectly and attributed to his parents rather than to John, as a step toward John being able to acknowledge and own his own concerns. This more gentle approach emphasizes the use of insight to build rather than to destroy self-esteem (Wachtel, 1993). Let us also consider the panther image: An elaborate theoretical symbol was developed, although that may or may not have been John's initial formulation when he saw the panther. However, through a combination of an empathic connection to John's dynamics and an ability to use suggestion that was effective because of the sound relationship that had been developed, John adopted the symbol as his own and used it in a constructive and meaningful manner (Wachtel, 1993).

This approach, as used by Wachtel, is closer to assimilative psychodynamic integration than any of the others. It begins with the same central concern for relational psychotherapy and then uses a wide variety of interventions, emphasizing the cyclical nature of the change process.

Assimilative Integration

In assimilative integration, a clear adherence to a single psychotherapeutic orientation is present, but techniques drawn from other orientations are integrated in as seamless a fashion as possible. Although there is variation in the home theory that different theorists have adopted, the example to be given is from assimilative psychodynamic integration (Gold & Stricker, 2001; Stricker & Gold, 1996). It is a case of mine that has not previously been published.

> Oscar is an 82-year-old man who I saw weekly for almost a year. He was married to Pearl for close to 60 years, almost every one of them unhappy. They have an adult son, Danny, who Oscar felt very responsible for because Danny has had a long series of psychiatric hospitalizations and, although he now is ambulatory, represented a continuing source of concern. Oscar did not speak easily about

affectionate feelings for Danny, or for most anyone else, but seemed to be more than simply concerned for his son. Oscar still was employed meaningfully in a sales position and had a history of good business success, devalued in his mind because it was accomplished in Pearl's family's business and the family was not properly appreciative of his contributions. Oscar is very bright and articulate, but his inability to do as well as he thought he should have in his academic experiences made this, too, an area in which he underestimated himself. He also had not been very comfortable socially, although he now seems to have a fairly active social life, engaging in a series of avocational activities with many acquaintances.

Oscar was not clear as to why he sought treatment. He indicated that he had been reminiscing and this produced many angry feelings, along with a concern that he had never become the person he might have been. He currently is taking an antidepressant, prescribed by a family physician, and felt much better than he had previously. Oscar had at least four previous therapeutic experiences, the most recent of which was a failed attempt at couples therapy, and this included two lengthy and unsuccessful psychoanalyses. He described all of his therapeutic experiences as unsuccessful and said he was very skeptical about what might be accomplished, but still was unclear as to what he wished to accomplish or why he was seeking treatment yet again. He did begin by talking about his preoccupation in his reminiscing with themes of sex and violence and then launched into an autobiographical account of his lifetime of unhappiness, loneliness, isolation, and perceived lack of success. He described his father as a distant and uninvolved man who never had time for him, his mother as a sweet and caring but ineffectual woman with no intellectual interests, and his older sister, now deceased, as relatively uninvolved with him, but a favorite of his father. He also had a younger sister, also now deceased, who was severely handicapped physically, thereby consuming what little attention there was in the family for a child.

When Oscar talked about sex and violence, his main focus was on violence, and this was on his inability to express the murderous impulses he felt toward others, particularly those who treated him in a demeaning and humiliating way. When he felt an impulse to retaliate, he also felt that he was on the verge of a panic attack, and so he backed away from action and inhibited whatever inclination he might have had toward a sense of agency in his life. There was a continuing contrast between his actual talent and success and his perceived ineptitude and failure. Any attempt to move in the direction of greater ability at self-expression was met with surprise that it might be possible and reluctance to make any attempts, but it seemed clear that violence, for Oscar, was synonymous with assertiveness. He did not even mind his inaction but would have liked to perceive it as a choice rather than as a sign of cowardice. There also was a sense, mingled with his wish to be more of a center of attention, that he was afraid of that fantasy becoming true because it would only lead, ultimately, to his being uncovered as the fraud that he was certain he is. Whatever current success he had, and was willing to acknowledge, during this treatment episode he attributed to the medication and surely not to anything he had done.

When Oscar turned to a consideration of his sexual preoccupation, there was similar talk of his failures. He described himself as being in a loveless and sexless marriage, and of having a history of unattractiveness, premature ejaculation, rejection, and little satisfaction. He has had a series of affairs for the past 30 years, including two separate ones currently, and the recent couples therapy was precipitated when Pearl finally discovered that this was going on, largely because Danny had betrayed a confidence. Nonetheless, she stayed with him and he continued the affair, only more discreetly. His main wish in a current sexual relationship was for someone who would care for, protect, and nurture him; physical expression is nice and satisfying (largely to his self-concept), but the main value of the affairs always had been the sense of acceptance, comfort, safety, and nurturance that it conveyed. His initial concern about his preoccupation with sex masked his need for acceptance, just as his initial concern about his preoccupation with violence masked his wish for assertiveness, and both reflected his feeling of inadequacy and humiliation.

Oscar's response to previous treatment focused on a single comment made by an analyst 50 years ago, when he was told that he was incapable of loving. This strikes me as a gross misperception and one that ignored the armor Oscar had built against being hurt again, an armor that kept him from making commitments or getting involved, which, in turn, is a pattern that reinforces his view of himself as unlovable and hopelessly inadequate. Oscar said that I, as compared to his previous therapists, seemed to try harder and to be more tuned in to him. He described me as kind, supportive, and probably a good deal smarter than I seemed, but also added that I had no penetrating insights.

Oscar's relating of a series of life events that led to disappointment, and his characteristic closing of a session with a wish that he had added something to my life, underlined his intellectualized need for reassurance and made clear the importance of examining our relationship as a microcosm of his characteristic relationships. I expressed a wish that I would not disappoint him as others had done. He frequently asked what insights I could provide for him and what I proposed to do for him. He seemed astonished when I stated that I couldn't give him any further insight, but that I might be able to mitigate his sense of being awful and to provide him with a relationship with a person who liked and respected him. He likened this to a massage, which feels good but is short-lived, and I suggested that perhaps he could learn how to massage himself. Although he dismissed this way of looking at treatment, he also had dismissed any prior attempts I made to provide understanding, usually by describing my interpretive comments as facile or simply a good paraphrase. He did say that he felt that, no matter what terrible thing he told me, I would find a way of identifying the redeeming features in it, but he did not state this in a complimentary fashion.

When I asked Oscar if I could present this case at a meeting, he immediately agreed, adding that it might be his only chance at fame. However, he returned to this topic many times in later sessions. First, he asked if he would hear what others said and was astonished by the thought that anyone would be foolish enough to focus on a single approach to understanding him. Recently, he asked why I had chosen him to present, and I described the nature of psychotherapy integration and the meeting at which I presented his case. He again fastened on his disappointment that there would be no epiphanies and how, even if I were successful in what I provided, he would need to find a perfect person outside of treatment to provide the same thing for him. I described how he might become more self-accepting and reduce the barriers he put up to relationships, a tendency he denied at first. However, his description of what he wanted from a woman was remarkably childlike in its wish for nurturance, and this recognition led him to talk about his stunted emotional growth. He has not yet seen how he wants this same primitive acceptance from me but did leave the last session with a statement that he never had been allowed to be a little boy, stated with some bravado, but with a catch in his throat.

This was a difficult case for me. Consistent with a relational approach to psychotherapy, I usually function in a way that adds understanding, and yet that approach did not seem to be promising or effective with Oscar. In addition, I usually intervene at the level of behavior, affect, cognition, and dynamics, but with Oscar, his behavior, despite his perception, did not seem markedly impaired, he resisted any attempt to reframe it, and dynamic interventions were not particularly effective, nor historically have they been effective for him. This left me with the need for affective interventions, which were scary to Oscar, as he much preferred the penetrating but unproductive insights that were more intellectually comfortable and less threatening. However, they did prove to be the only approach that provided Oscar with something that was new for him and effective in reaching the barrier he had established against any connection with others. In working with Oscar, it also was necessary to keep his age in mind, as this presented issues concerning long-ingrained patterns as well as a more limited view of what the long term held. It also allowed for the integration of the use of reminiscence therapy (Butler, 1963), an approach with older adults that is quite useful.

Client-Directed Psychotherapy

This approach may be the one most likely to be added to the current classification scheme. In this approach, the preferences of the client drive the therapeutic course, rather than the preferences of the therapist or the dictates of theory. The case of Richard is an example of what Gold refers to as client-initiated integration (Gold, 2006) and is an example of this approach as practiced by a prominent integrationist with a clear psychodynamic bent.

"Richard was a White single man in his mid-20s who sought therapy for what he described as mild but chronic depression, a variety of anxiety symptoms that he did not initially specify, and difficulties in sustaining intimate relationships with women" (p. 255). He was a schoolteacher in a suburban area where his family also lived. He recently had become engaged to Patricia, and she encouraged him to seek treatment because of his depression.

Richard was sufficiently sophisticated about psychology that he asked for and received a referral for twice weekly therapy with a psychodynamic practitioner. It had a relatively uneventful course in which insight was gained and led to a relief of the depression and an improved relationship with Patricia. It also moved his anxiety to the forefront, and he discussed several near-phobic experiences and performance anxiety in several areas, including sexual. This changed the nature of the therapy, as a positive working relationship seemed to worsen. When this topic was introduced, Richard indicated that insight was not as helpful with anxiety as it had been with depression, and he raised the possibility of cognitive–behavioral therapy as a possible alternative.

Richard's initial reluctance to raise the issue of therapeutic approach with his therapist until it was invited was linked to his relationship with a father who did not tolerate disagreement. However, rather than follow this transferential lead, Gold chose to shift to a more cognitive–behavioral mode of treatment. Some of the techniques were familiar to Richard, who attempted to use them on the basis of his reading, but he had not succeeded. However, with the therapist's support and a reinstitution of the positive therapeutic relationship, the techniques became more helpful and progress was made with the anxiety symptoms.

Therapy then proceeded with shifts between psychodynamic and cognitive–behavioral interventions, with the flow dictated by the client. Interestingly, at one point Richard suggested the use of an experiential intervention, chair work for his relationship with his father, and then berated the therapist for not thinking of it first. Rather than behaving defensively or interpretively, Gold acknowledged the countertransference inherent in his failure to take the lead, and the subsequent sessions proved very productive, both in dealing with the parental relationship and repairing and solidifying the therapeutic alliance.

The final stages of therapy were concerned with Richard's performance anxiety, particularly as it related to sexual functioning. The therapist thought that Richard's unacknowledged anger toward Patricia was central, whereas he was more interested in specific technical interventions. Finally, Gold complied and referred Richard and Patricia to a sex therapist to work on the problem, as Richard had requested. However, that therapist also raised the question about Richard's anger, and he then was willing to deal with it. The referral avoided a power struggle and led to a productive exploration of the dynamic issue at a point where Richard was willing to do that.

The therapy with Richard might easily be seen as an example of assimilative integration, and Gold is well known for his work in this area (Gold & Stricker, 2001). The distinction in this case is that the integrative shifts were initiated by the client rather than the therapist, and this change in the power structure of the relationship was crucial to the progress of the treatment. Particularly in light of Richard's conflicted relationship with an authoritarian father, Gold's willingness to allow Richard to take the lead provided a corrective emotional experience that was central to the therapeutic success that was achieved. A client without Richard's experience with and sophistication about psychotherapy would not have been as capable of directing the treatment, but most clients have an implicit sense of what they do and do not find helpful. It usually is useful to be responsive to these expressed needs (Duncan, Sparks, & Miller, 2006).

Diversity

The appropriate consideration of diversity poses a serious problem throughout the entire field of psychotherapy (Sue, 1998) and, unfortunately, psychotherapy integration is only somewhat better than the field as a whole. On the surface, it does appear that psychotherapy integration would be in a good position to respond effectively to diversity because of the flexibility that is demonstrated in most integrative approaches and the lack of the straitjacket that many more rigid theoretical applications seem to embody. However, a look at the major compendia in psychotherapy integration (Norcross & Goldfried, 1992, 2005a; Stricker & Gold, 1993, 2006a) reveals few cases involving members of ethnically or culturally different groups. This, by itself, is not a problem but is a reflection of the failure of many theories to take cultural considerations into account. There are some important exceptions to this trend, as will be outlined below.

There is a representation within psychotherapy integration cases as to age, gender, and sexual orientation, among other areas, but not as to ethnicity and culture. The major exceptions to this generalization are works that specifically target these groups (Franklin, Carter, & Grace, 1993; Ivey & Brooks-Harris, 2005) rather than within broader examples of psychotherapy integration. Franklin and colleagues (1993) present many short examples of the relevance of ethnicity, particularly African-American ethnicity, to psychotherapy. Ivey and Brooks-Harris (2005) have an elaborately worked-out approach to working with diverse clients based on identity stages, developmental levels, and focal dimensions, with different theoretical approaches seen as appropriate at different stages. Their techniques resemble the work of Prochaska (Prochaska & DiClemente, 2005) on stages of therapy and also the work of Beutler (Beutler & Clarkin, 1990) on therapeutic matching. This being the case, within the current system, the best classification for the work of Ivey and Brooks-Harris would be within technical integration. The case of Pono (Ivey & Brooks-Harris, 2005) is illustrative of using this system with a client who demonstrates a varied set of diverse characteristics.

"Pono is a 25-year-old, gay, Hawaiian male. After attending college and working for a couple of years in Chicago, he moved back to Hawaii 1 year ago. Pono consulted with a physician because he was having trouble sleeping and because he frequently felt 'jittery and uptight.' The physician referred Pono to Dr. K. for psychotherapy. Pono began meeting with Dr. K., a heterosexual, Japanese-American, male psychologist in his mid-fifties. Pono told Dr. K. that he had been experiencing symptoms of anxiety and depression since moving back to Hawaii. Pono was surprised at this reaction because, when he was living on the mainland, he frequently dreamed of returning home and hoped he would feel more comfortable back in Hawaii. Pono attended a total of 18 sessions of individual psychotherapy during a 6 month time span" (p. 331).

After a multidimensional inquiry into the situation, Dr. K. determined that Pono was having difficulty with the transition from Chicago to Hawaii. Pono felt he didn't fit in when he was in Hawaii, a feeling he also had in Chicago. This led to feelings of loneliness, despair, and agitation. Dr. K. concluded that, in Chicago, Pono was out of place as a Hawaiian but could explore being gay; in Hawaii, he was comfortable as a Hawaiian but out of place as a gay man. On the basis of this formulation, Dr. K. developed a matching treatment plan that focused on feelings and interpersonal patterns with regard to cultural identity, but on thoughts and actions with regard to sexual orientation.

Dr. K. encouraged a therapeutic relationship built on warmth and also on his status as a wise elder, taking advantage of Pono's cultural inclinations. He also affirmed Pono's gay identity, an unusual experience for Pono coming from a heterosexual man. Dr. K. pointed out the similarity between the difficulty with racism in Chicago and heterosexism in Hawaii. Thus, Pono could be comfortably gay in one setting and comfortably Hawaiian in another, but was having trouble blending both parts of his identity in one setting. An experiential two-chair approach helped Pono to recognize the difficulty he was having in this regard and how the difficulty was contextual.

The next step in treatment was to help Pono to find a context in which both parts of his identity could feel comfortable. After some discussion, it was determined that this might occur in a hula dance setting. There, Pono could act as a Hawaiian, express himself in a familiar and welcome physical manner, and find people who were more comfortable with his gay identity. When Pono did this, he made several new friends, some of whom were openly gay. Then, with Dr. K.'s help, Pono was able to come out himself, reconciling the Hawaiian–gay split he had experienced. After doing this successfully, Pono contemplated coming out to his family and did so after therapy had terminated successfully.

This case illustrates many components of a culturally informed integrative treatment. The treatment was guided by a knowledge and acceptance of Pono's dual cultural identities, as a Hawaiian and as a gay man, each of which had caused him anxiety in different settings. This differs from assimilative psychodynamic integration in that there is no central psychological theory that guides the work. However, as is characteristic of technical integration, many different interventions were used. Interventions were taken from psychodynamic (focusing on feelings and interpersonal patterns), behavioral (encouraging adaptive activities), and experiential (two-chair work) traditions, and each contributed to the overall success of the treatment. In addition, it should be noted that here, as in many successful therapies, the value of the treatment extends beyond the termination of the therapeutic relationship, as Pono did not begin to discuss his sexual identity with his family until after therapy had ended.

ROLE OF THERAPIST–CLIENT RELATIONSHIP

The therapist–client relationship is central to assimilative psychodynamic integration, to most other approaches to psychotherapy integration, and to most single school approaches to psychotherapy. Taking assimilative psychodynamic integration first, the treatment approach is similar in many ways to relational psychodynamic psychotherapy. The relationship between the therapist and the client are of foremost concern, and much that is mutative is seen as arising in the therapeutic relationship. The relationship is seen as a microcosm of all of the client's relationships, and so understanding the client's patterns with the therapist helps to illuminate similar patterns with others, both as they were created in the past and are repeated in the present. The client always seeks enactments, or repetitions of past patterns of interacting, which are familiar and comfortable even if they are, at the same time, maladaptive. It is the task of the therapist to recognize this pattern, to resist the enactment, and, by doing so, to provide a corrective emotional experience (Alexander & French, 1946).

The therapeutic task is not completed with the provision of the corrective emotional experience. The client may feel more comfortable and safe within the relationship, but the goal of psychotherapy is not simply to make the client comfortable with the therapist. This is the beginning of an effort to generalize the possibilities of varying patterns of relating and to encourage the client to try out various new relationships, always preparing him for the possibility that the new approach may not work as well outside the treatment room as it does within. In this phase of treatment, integration begins to play a large role, as homework, role playing, and suggestion are added to the range of interventions open to the therapist. The impetus for change occurs in the therapeutic relationship, but the fulfillment occurs outside the treatment room and often requires an active therapist. In this attempt, the concept of attachment (Bowlby, 1980) is a valuable one. The client is best able to explore and experiment away from the therapist after having achieved a secure attachment relationship to the therapist so that strength can be garnered for the experimentation with new activities, and there is reassurance that even failures in these experiments will not threaten the client with a loss of regard from the therapist.

Finally, with regard to assimilative psychodynamic integration, it is important to remember that this system is based on the three-tier theory of personality (Gold & Stricker, 1993; Stricker & Gold, 1988). Any intervention at any level will reverberate throughout all the tiers, and the relational intervention at Tier 3 is likely to have important repercussions at the behavioral (Tier 1) and cognitive (Tier 2) levels. Similarly, these behavioral and cognitive changes are likely to shed further light on Tier 3 issues and promote further appreciation of the importance of understanding dynamics for the client.

For other approaches to psychotherapy integration, the therapeutic relationship also is important, but the use of the relationship differs. In some approaches, particularly if they are based in more cognitive–behavioral home schools, the relationship is the foundation on which any progress must be built. Thus, for a technical integrationist such as Lazarus (2005), a sound relationship is necessary for the impact of the interventions that follow to be effective. For integrationist efforts with clearer roots in psychodynamic thought (Allen, 2006), the relationship can be the vehicle through which change occurs, much as has been described previously for the impact of a corrective emotional experience. Within theoretical integration, the role of the relationship will depend on the theories being integrated, but will follow the pattern just noted, so that the relationship either is a foundation or a vehicle for successful treatment.

For the common factors approach, the therapeutic relationship, particularly a sound therapeutic alliance, appears on almost any list of potential common factors (Grencavage & Norcross, 1990). For example, the outcome-informed approach to psychotherapy integration (Miller, Duncan, & Hubble, 2005) has the therapeutic bond as one of the major pillars on which a successful treatment is built.

Role of Therapist

It is difficult to separate the role of the therapist from the therapist–client relationship discussed previously. However, the therapist engages in activities that are not related to relationship building, so these interventions will be the focus of this discussion. In general, therapists can be more or less active. The closer the therapist is to a cognitive–behavioral approach, the more active she is likely to be, whereas more psychodynamically inclined practitioners are more likely to be less active. The integrative therapist is likely to be less active than a strict cognitive–behavioral therapist and more active than a strict psychodynamic therapist.

Beginning with assimilative psychodynamic integration, the therapist acts in typical psychodynamic ways, listening carefully, intervening occasionally, and using those interventions as a means of increasing the range of appreciation of the client for external and internal patterns (Tier 3). However, true to the model, this reduced activity is supplemented by several active interventions chosen from cognitive–behavioral and experiential orientations. These interventions are meant to encourage specific behaviors (Tier 1) and to increase the appreciation of thought patterns and feelings (Tier 2). Wherever the intervention occurs, it will increase the likelihood of change at other tiers as well, through the interrelated nature of the tiers.

The activity of the therapist involved with theoretical integration depends on the theories that are being integrated and the predominance of one theory or the other in the integration. Cyclical psychodynamics (Wachtel, 1997), although it integrates behavioral approaches, is an approach with deep roots in relational psychodynamic thinking, and the activity of the therapist is similar to the therapist in assimilative psychodynamic integration. In contrast, the integrative therapist practicing cognitive behavioral analysis system of psychotherapy (CBASP; McCullough, 2000) is more likely to take a more active role in the treatment, making clear suggestions and developing an active treatment plan that depends on an assessment of the client's developmental history. Systematic measurement is an important component of CBASP and helps to involve the client actively in the course of treatment.

The outcome-informed approach to common factors integration (Miller et al., 2005) also relies heavily on the process of ongoing assessment. The therapist in this model is usually quite active but takes her cue from the client in determining the treatment plan. Finally, there is technical integration, where the description of the therapist taking her cue from the client is again appropriate. In all of these approaches, there are times for activity and times for relative inactivity, and it is the client who determines which is more appropriate at any particular time. This is in contrast to a more single school approach where the theory rather than the therapeutic relationship and client characteristics determine the nature of therapist activity.

Role of Client

Just as it is difficult to separate the role of the therapist from the therapeutic relationship, there are some difficulties in doing that with the client. However, here there are some distinctions that are worth considering. In virtually every form of therapy, the needs of the client should be primary. In cognitive–behavioral therapy and with its integrative variants, the therapist actively designs a treatment plan but does so in response to the stated needs of the client. In psychodynamic therapy and with its integrative variants, the therapist is less active, listening carefully to the client before intervening with an interpretation or a request for a clarification. In both these approaches, the therapist takes her cue from the client before responding in a manner characteristic of the approach.

Having stated this general principle, let us look more carefully at the specific therapeutic approaches within psychotherapy integration. In assimilative psychodynamic integration (Gold & Stricker, 2001; Stricker & Gold, 1996), the critical issue of the therapeutic relationship as a microcosm of the client's manner of relating places the client at center stage, with the therapist being responsive to the client, both with traditional listening techniques and with more active interventions as required. Gold's case of Richard (Gold, 2006), presented previously in this chapter, is a fine example of a blend of assimilative psychodynamic integration and the client-directed approach. Although the case of Richard is an example of the client actively suggesting approaches, the general assimilative psychodynamic integrationist will allow the client to do the same thing in a less explicit manner. Instead, the client's needs implicitly dictate the strategies of therapy and specific interventions that are chosen.

The common factors approach often highlights the centrality of the client to the therapeutic process. In Frank's (1961) landmark work, several client-centered common factors are cited. These include the arousal of hope and affective involvement in the client and the client's expectation of change. Beitman (Beitman et al., 2005; Beitman et al., 2006), in emphasizing the future expectations of the client as an organizing common factor, again places the client front and center in the design of therapeutic interventions. The tendency to emphasize the client is made most explicit in the outcome-informed approach (Duncan et al., 2006; Miller et al., 2005). Here, much as in Gold's (2006) example, the client is far more active in indicating a theory of change and a consequent set of interactions that will be effective. By doing this, the client's hope for and expectation of change are increased, bringing us back full circle to the suggestions of common factors made by Frank (1961).

In technical integration, it clearly must be the client who dictates the interventions that the therapist, in order to be responsive to presenting problems and concerns, will choose. For Lazarus and multimodal therapy (2005), a BASIC-ID evaluation is used to point to particular areas that are in need of interventions; from this initial assessment, a treatment plan and set of interventions can be designed. For Beutler and his prescriptive therapy (Beutler, Consoli, & Lane, 2005; Beutler et al., 2006), a formal evaluation also begins the therapeutic process and indicates the type of treatment that will be initiated. In both cases, the clear pattern is to assess the client and then determine which of a large number of possible approaches or interventions are most likely to be effective with the specific client.

It is more difficult to summarize theoretical integration because the approach depends on the particular set of theories that are being integrated. Where the nature of the integration relies heavily on a psychodynamic approach (Wachtel, 1997), the client is relied on to indicate areas of concern and typical methods of dealing with those concerns. The therapist initially is relatively quiet and responsive, allowing a good alliance to develop, and then introduces more active interventions as the client's progress indicates that they may be needed and useful. For a more cognitive–behaviorally grounded approach (Fensterheim, 1993), the emphasis and direction may be reversed, but the same alternation of passive listening, relationship building, and active intervening is conducted. Here, the relationship is established as a foundation for the work, interventions are introduced quickly, and more interpretive work with patterns of behavior is reserved for introduction at a later point, if necessary.

Of course, the clearest example of the role of the client is present in the integrative effort known as client-directed therapy (Duncan et al., 2006; Miller et al., 2005). Here, it is the client who suggests a theory of change and the best path to reach that change. The therapist follows the client's lead, choosing techniques that will accomplish the agreed-upon goals. It is interesting to ask whether this approach is not also followed, without using the client-directed terminology, by technical integrationists and, in fact, by therapists of any persuasion, all of whom presumably move toward mutually established goals using techniques dictated by the theory or approach of the therapist.

BRIEF AND LONG-TERM STRATEGIES/TECHNIQUES

The strategies and techniques used in psychotherapy integration depend on the goals and orientation of the specific approach being used. Generally, the more linked to psychodynamic theory the approach, the more long term the strategy, whereas the more cognitive–behavioral the approach, the more short term the strategy. However, short-term strategies have been adopted by psychodynamic approaches (Messer & Warren, 1995), and some cognitive–behavioral approaches have found the need to extend to longer term treatment (Young, 1999). The more basic principle is not linked to orientation as much as it is to goal. The more symptom-focused the treatment is (and cognitive–behavioral as well as some family approaches can be described this way), the more short term the treatment is likely to be. The more the treatment focuses on personality change and other existential issues (psychodynamic and experiential treatments usually do this), the more long term the treatment is likely to be. In general, there is a dose–effect relationship in psychotherapy (Howard, Kopta, Krause, & Orlinsky, 1986): Many clients show symptom change within a fairly brief (8–16 sessions) period of time, more show change as treatment lengthens, and changes in factors other than symptoms may well take a good deal longer.

Thus, the more the goal of treatment is specific and symptom-oriented, the more likely it is that short-term treatment strategies will be effective.

Goal setting thus can be identified as a major approach to determining whether short- or long-term strategies are more likely to be effective. Another such strategy is client selection. Long-term treatment requires a certain amount of ego strength, or resilience, for the client to engage in the necessary introspection and tolerate the likely anxiety that will be aroused. Short-term approaches are not likely to be used with clients who are severely disturbed, have serious personality disorders, have addictive problems or impulse disorders, or are suicidal (Messer, Sanderson, & Gurman, 2003).

The strategies of the more short-term treatments, of course, do not need to be modified for a short-term approach. Thus, I will concentrate on how the long-term therapist should modify treatment in order to practice in a more short-term model. Two important parameters already have been identified. The goal of treatment must be established and is likely to be concentrated on symptom alleviation. The client must be carefully selected, and those chosen will be healthier and more motivated for change. Of course, a time limit often is part of the initial orientation toward treatment. The goal that is established becomes a focus of treatment, and other issues, as interesting or important as they may seem to be, are set aside in favor of the central focus. The therapist is more active than generally is the case in longer-term treatment, and this activity is required to keep the focus salient and the treatment moving along. The active offering of empathy also is a useful technique to be adopted by the short-term therapist.

Several integrative approaches take a specific short-term approach. It should be noted that one of the earliest approaches to reduce the time of psychodynamic treatment was in the recommendation for a corrective emotional experience (Alexander & French, 1946), and this has been mentioned many times as a central feature of many integrative therapies. Within the classification of technical integration, Beutler (Beutler et al., 2005; Beutler et al., 2006) has established the intensity of treatment as a specific matching variable within his prescriptive approach. Much as has already been detailed, more seriously disturbed clients require more intensive treatments and are not good candidates for short-term approaches. Wolfe's

(2005) theoretically integrative approach begins with a short-term focus on anxiety, and interventions are designed to reduce the target symptom. After symptom change is accomplished, if the client expresses an interest in further exploration, the therapist moves on to a longer-term approach to heal the wounded self. Here again, the symptom can be treated briefly, but the more personality-related problem requires longer treatment. Ryle (Ryle & Low, 1993) has developed a theoretically integrated approach and, in order to conform to the requirements of the health care delivery system in Great Britain, an intensive treatment is rendered in a fairly short period of time. This requirement of third party payers generally has led to briefer approaches to treatment, and this is as true within psychotherapy integration as it is for psychotherapy in general.

A Long-Term Case: Robert

This case is an example of assimilative psychodynamic integration with a long-term client who presented with a complicated issue concerning sexual identification. It is one of my cases and has not been published previously.

I saw Robert on a once-weekly basis in extended psychotherapy. Let me begin by reproducing, verbatim, the notes that I took after the very first session:

Robert is a 40-year-old man, married to Gail for more than 20 years, with three teenage children, but separated from her for four years while having an affair with a woman named Ronnie. His presenting problem is cross-dressing, which he feels occurs during times of depression, which are frequent and can be serious. He has a long history of heavy drinking up until five years ago when he joined AA. The primary theme that emerged was a profound sense of inadequacy and low self-esteem, accompanied by severe interpersonal discomfort. He described three heads—he can be male when he is involved with work or macho hobbies, or he dresses up like a woman, or he wears diapers, which he views as self-humiliation. Sexually, he has had a long history of lack of gratification until the affair with Ronnie, and even there the gratification is not as a man making love to a woman, but through fantasies as yet undescribed. The dressing is not accompanied by sexual satisfaction and seems to be a reflection of his tendency to hide. He described the dressing as dating to pre-school days; his mother died when he was seven, and he lived with his father and grandparents and felt frightened unless he cross-dressed. He was painfully shy and afraid of humiliation and has always, until now, worked with partners who did the talking for him. He was always given to fantasy, particularly of an abortive love for Liz (an early object of his affections), but unable to act except in counterphobic macho ways. He also hid behind alcohol and now under his covers in the morning. His accomplishments are many, his ability seems great, but his appreciation is very limited, and AA is beginning to wear off, which may frighten him.

Thus, at the end of one session I knew that Robert was a depressed transvestite, a reformed alcoholic, a man with a marriage on the verge of dissolving, a man feeling so inadequate and so withdrawn that he had difficulty functioning, and a person who had been subject to a profound early loss. In the early part of the treatment I also learned that he had been abandoned by his father shortly after his mother's death, was still living at home with Gail despite their estrangement, and had no relationship to speak of with his children or his family of origin. In addition, his business was foundering despite his working 7 days a week, 16 hours a day, because of his reluctance to return the calls of potential customers or to ask for payment. I also learned that he was a man of remarkable native ability and a clear motivation to improve. He had a sound relationship with Ronnie, herself a troubled woman, and a network of friends who cared for him, although he found this difficult to believe or trust.

By the end of treatment, Robert did not experience serious depression, although he still was prone to discouragement. He had not had a drink since the beginning of therapy and had not worn diapers or women's clothing after he first stopped doing so. He obtained a divorce from Gail and married Ronnie, a relationship that appeared to be a great source of satisfaction to him. His children remained somewhat distant, but he developed a much better relationship with them, and even planned on taking his son into his business. He began a contact with his now-elderly father, and that, too, seemed positive but limited. He reduced his work schedule to about 5 and a half days, 10 hours a day, took regular time off, and cleared a long-standing debt to the IRS. The business functioned well and he contemplated, with some pleasure, the time that he could turn it over to his son and then retire to a home he and Ronnie purchased in Pennsylvania, where he would act as a consultant and do odd jobs as he chose. Clearly, at the start of treatment he was a seriously impaired man, and he made significant progress during the course of treatment. How did this all come about?

Generally, my approach to treatment is guided by a psychodynamic understanding of the client, and I see understanding, for myself and the client, to be integral to the success of the treatment. I also recognize that behavior is more easily changed by techniques not rooted in understanding. Whether understanding promotes behavior change or behavior change promotes understanding can be debated, and I suspect good examples can be found for each sequence. I usually feel an obligation to clients to integrate these behavioral techniques into the treatment to help them with the issues that often bring them to treatment. An interesting pattern developed with Robert and was repeated many times during the treatment. He would show some marked symptomatic improvement, recognize that he was doing much better, but complain that he didn't feel any better. He became a psychodynamic conscience, asking me for understanding so that he could master the situation and placing his feelings above his actions, even when strikingly disabling symptoms were involved. Whether he learned this orientation from me or not, and we can attribute it to positive transference or modeling as we choose, it raises the important question as to the extent to which changes in well-being track changes in behavior, and which of the two deserve priority.

From the earliest point in treatment, I conceptualized Robert's primary problem as lying in the area of self-esteem, rather than with any of his dramatic symptoms. His mother was a relatively cold and controlling woman, and when she developed cancer, she became far more difficult. She often would humiliate him by tying him up or by painting his fingernails, and his escape would be by putting on her underwear, fantasizing that he was Superman, and withdrawing from her. This provided an early model of his sensitivity to embarrassment, identification with the aggressor, withdrawal into fantasy, and use of women's clothing as a source of gratification. He often felt badly as an adult, used dressing as an escape from these bad feelings, and found it to be reinforcing. Thus, to take dressing away from him before reducing the bad feelings about himself probably would have increased his depression; it might not even have been possible. Robert referred to himself as Roberta when he dressed, experienced the only good feelings he had as Roberta, and initially resented any sense he had from me that Roberta was a gimmick to bring about a feeling state, rather than a genuine and preferred personage. My notes from the sixteenth session read:

Robert was very upset, feeling that I didn't understand him last week and he was going nowhere. He blamed this on himself, decided to abandon Roberta for the week, and felt very empty. It is clear that any judgmental comments will be harmful, and that he can understand an integration of Robert and Roberta as a distant goal, but in an intermediate frame he can only function comfortably as Roberta.

Belongingness was very important to Robert, and he only felt he fit as a woman, perhaps because his male self had such a history of feeling rejected and out of place. The early part of treatment, therefore, was spent on his work and his relationships. Work was a source of occasional satisfaction and pride to him, when he did not sabotage it. He also came to see how he expected to be rejected by others and then made it a self-fulfilling prophecy by acting in a way that produced the rejection he feared, but felt he deserved. In this arena, as in some others, I took a directive stance that I would not with regard to Roberta, encouraging specific actions to break the cycle of rejection he often produced. Another early directive intervention was to encourage him to see a lawyer, an action that would relieve him of some of his hopelessness, get him away from the destructive relationship with Gail, and promote the relationship with Ronnie.

My encouragement of various acts served as permission for him and approval of a change he could not bring himself to make on his own, although it also was a striking deviation from a psychodynamic approach. It also produced an interesting offshoot: Because I was willing to be directive, but did not take sides about Roberta, he felt he had permission to explore the limits of that personage and to make choices rather than feel trapped by her. He varied between renouncing Roberta for short periods of time and coming to sessions in makeup, pointing out that he was wearing a bra under his work shirt.

One of the early approaches to treatment was a continuous focus on his feelings, an area in which he felt blocked and unfamiliar. His predominant feeling was anger, bordering on rage, which he felt very uncomfortable about and often turned against himself. The blockage of feelings was massive and also led him to restrict any possibility of feeling good, lest allowing feelings into consciousness would turn into the fury he feared.

In the eighth month of treatment, Robert signed a separation agreement, a first step toward emancipation. He also reduced his work schedule somewhat, but found that he felt bored and worthless when he wasn't productive. I then encouraged his trips to Pennsylvania, where he was able to feel good, although often it was in the form of Roberta. He then was able to put Roberta into words, seeing women as more free from responsibility and more able to attend to their own needs rather than taking care of others, an interesting deviation from the usual stereotype that probably resulted from the role reversal he experienced when he had to take care of his dying mother. Shortly after this verbalization, he began to speak of the feminine side of Robert, rather than personalizing it as Roberta. Robert then was even able to refer to some good feelings without the need to characterize them as female.

Next, Robert began to speak of his father and children. He and his father seemed to have good feelings for each other, but these were never expressed and Robert always felt unworthy and at fault. It was important, although it came much later, for him to recognize that his father's early rejection of him may have been due to his father's failings rather than to Robert's own deficiencies. He also felt good about his children but was convinced that he was a bad and neglectful father, as his had been, and so he did not pursue any relationship with them. His father lived at some distance, so it did not seem like a productive path to encourage that relationship, but his children were available and I encouraged an opening of some dialogue with them. He was able to do things for them, but without much satisfaction, since he did not feel that he was being genuine about it. At this same time I encouraged him to find a hobby and to buy some land in Pennsylvania, both of which would add to some sense of a gratified self. He chose building models as his hobby, but this also failed, as did the dialogue with his children, because it was premature. However, the land was bought and proved a great source of satisfaction for him. This underlines the difficulty and the advantage of directive interventions: When they are good, they are very, very good, since they promote and give sanction to growth, but when they are bad, they are horrid, since they also take some autonomy from the client.

Treatment continued in a relatively traditional exploratory way, mixed with occasional directives, until the point when I either incorporated other techniques or deviated from psychodynamic ones and expressed clearly to him how positively I felt about him. He was touched almost to the point of tears, and this began a period in which he examined some of the reasons why he could not be as close to me, Ronnie, or his children as he would like. Shortly after this, he told his children about Ronnie, and he told them that he loved them. He also mentioned having an old photo album that might reawaken some of his early memories. Since that time, he has increased his memory for the early days by astronomic proportions but, despite my encouragement, has yet to bring the album into a session, since this still holds a strange measure of terror for him. It was also about this time that Ronnie became discouraged by Robert's persistent difficulties, and he often came in convinced that she would leave him, only to have me encourage him not to withdraw from her as he usually would. He found that he was able to repair their relationship.

Although Robert was still dressing, it had become something Robert did rather than a way of becoming Roberta. The depression that had characterized his earlier failures had become disgust, an unpleasant sense of failure, but not a catastrophic one. Shortly after this, he acknowledged that he never really realized how important it was that his mother died and how much he missed what she might have done for him. He remembered happy times before she became ill and thought that he might be trying to preserve her through her superficial characteristics, such as dress. He then began to see dressing as a way of affirming his worth rather than a way of producing it and began to acknowledge the possibility that he may be the decent, able, caring person that I seemed to see, even if he didn't. It was important for him to feel that his past really mattered, that he spent a great deal of energy reliving it, and that people were neither his mother, who would abandon him, nor his father, who would reject him. Robert was now dressing but feeling more comfortable about it, interested in learning what it did for him, and interested in incorporating it within him. Interestingly, at about this time he stopped talking about dressing and shortly thereafter stopped doing it, but never discussed the decision to stop. After he was comfortable that dressing was a thing of the past, he did talk about it as similar to alcohol in that both provided him a way of not feeling bad and that he was able to stop them when he had other sources of feeling good.

He began to see his father and, although the meetings were somewhat distant and strained, they were not violent as he had feared. He also began to spend more time with his children and was able to respond in an appropriate and caring way when one of his daughters needed an abortion. He was at a stage where his feelings were beginning to emerge, and they were caring and appropriate but also very frightening to him, so that they were alternate sources of pleasure and withdrawal. His disbelief that anyone could have faith in him was followed by tears when I indicated that I did, and my general approach to his feelings was far more affirmative and self-revealing than would be typical in a psychodynamic approach. He often mentioned that it was difficult for him to hear me compliment him since he did not like being teased or exposed to potential ridicule, but he also was quite touched by these compliments and seemed to incorporate them into a slowly growing sense of himself.

When Robert announced that he and Ronnie were going to be married, he did not allow himself to feel good about it, as he had no belief that it would really happen. As the wedding approached, he was able to talk about his disbelief in good happening to him without the good being spoiled or taken away. He spoke of his terror about dependency, because he couldn't count on anyone, but also his resentment of doing for others as no one ever did for him. The situation was complicated by Ronnie's development of a serious back problem, requiring surgery, and convincing Robert that this dream, too, would be spoiled. Fortunately, she recovered nicely, the wedding occurred, and the marriage has been a satisfying one for both of them. Robert then focused more on growth than remediation. He still had ups and downs, but the downs were shorter, less deep, and further apart. He found a number of activities that were gratifying to him, improved his business, made realistic plans for the future, and looked forward to settling in Pennsylvania in the next few years. He even believed that the progress he made was largely due to his own efforts and abilities but was able to be grateful for my part in it. When I told him that I wanted to present his case at a meeting and asked his permission to discuss his treatment, he readily complied, indicated that he felt it as an affirmation of the progress he made, suggested that he hoped his experiences would be of value to others, and said that he felt it was important for people with problems like alcohol and sex to understand themselves, and not simply to change the symptom.

Before reviewing this case, it should be noted that Robert was first seen many years ago. His presenting issue, and one that is steeped in cultural difference, was cross-dressing. Both his attitudes and mine were necessarily based on the understanding of the time. Had he walked into my office today, both of us would have been more accepting of this behavior, and he may not have seen it as a problem to be changed. That different attitude might well have contributed to greater self-acceptance and made life much easier for him. In light of all the early family problems Robert experienced, he still might have come for therapy, but the presenting issues and subsequent focus would have been much different.

A great deal of material about Robert has been omitted in the interest of space, but this summary illustrates three techniques that were intermixed throughout. The first was a focus on feelings, which were initially foreign to Robert, with my response being as direct and open as possible, both to model an appropriate response and to help him to recognize that his feelings were not dangerous and would not frighten away someone who was important to him. Second, I assumed a somewhat directive role, much as a good father might, although it usually took the form of suggestions that left him the possibility of accepting or rejecting them. Finally, in an attempt to tie the past to the present, there was a significant use of metaphor, with his early experiences being used to symbolize many of his current interactions. For example, people who told him how good he is, promised him much, but did not deliver were reminiscent of his being told how talented he was, and always being promised a paint set, but never getting one. In this regard, it is of note that, during therapy, he began to take art lessons, finally giving himself the paints that he always had been denied. Another example of metaphor was his memory of, at age 7, accidentally squeezing the toothpaste out of the tube, trying to get it back in, and then excitedly going to his father with this story, only to be yelled at for being silly. This helped capture his current experience with being inhibited about being playful, and as a result he reduced his work schedule sharply and began to enjoy himself more.

There is no doubt that Robert did very well in treatment, and his strides were more than I would have predicted after that first session. How did this all happen? I am a great believer in understanding, and his grasp, through metaphor, of the relationship between the past and the present were important to him. Nonetheless, he often would say, "Now that I understand the connection, what do I do about it?" Given his presenting problem, behavior change was important to him, and this is a man who can be seen as improved in terms of the massive behavioral changes he made. Still, he frequently would say to me, "I can recognize how different

I am, and how much better I am doing, so why don't I feel better?" I feel that both his cognitive and behavioral changes were important, and each helped to reinforce the other. However, if I had to choose a single source of his benefit, I would opt for what Alexander and French (1946) referred to as a *corrective emotional experience*. The most crucial aspect of Robert's treatment was his gradual recognition of himself as an individual worthy of being valued. My response to him—listening without the ridicule he had come to expect from others, standing by him despite his clinging to what he regarded as symptoms, and allowing him to retain ego-syntonic actions even though he felt I did not endorse them—gave him a sense of himself as a person of worth who could make choices for himself. His feelings, filled with rage as they were, could be expressed without fear of punishment, and as he did so, he learned that they weren't quite as evil as he had suspected. As he began to grow emotionally, he saw corresponding behavioral changes and achieved a framework for understanding this growth and these changes so that it all came together as one meaningful whole. I suspect that Robert could have been helped somewhat by a sole focus on the affective, behavioral, or cognitive but would not have made the strides that he did without an integration of the three.

The case was introduced as an example of assimilative psychodynamic integration. The theoretical basis for my understanding of Robert was psychodynamic, and this was also technically present in the use of metaphor, the value of understanding, and the emphasis on the role of the past. However, the introduction of affect-arousing techniques was more consistent with an experiential approach, as was the active prizing in which I engaged. In addition, the heightened directiveness and assignment of homework came from a cognitive–behavioral orientation.

When I presented the case, one positive response characterized it as an example of "George" therapy rather than one specific to any particular orientation or integrative approach. In a way, all therapy is an individually determined "George" therapy, with a theoretical understanding and mixture of techniques delivered with a clear personal style that may enhance the therapeutic relationship and add effectiveness to whatever is being done. Rogers (1957, 1961) referred to this as genuineness and saw it as one of three necessary and sufficient conditions for therapeutic success.

OBSTACLES OR PROBLEMS USING THIS APPROACH

There are two separate issues to consider as potential obstacles or problems concerning psychotherapy integration. The first is rooted in the treatment and the difficulties that might occur in applying it to some clients or problems. The second is in the therapist and problems that might occur in learning and applying the approach of psychotherapy integration. The first problem we will consider is that related to the treatment.

Any approach to psychotherapy has problems and is not applicable to every client and every problem that may be presented. Psychotherapy integration is not immune from this problem. However, whereas many integrative approaches are necessarily limited in scope, psychotherapy integration as a process has much wider application because it seeks the best treatment for each presenting issue. In addition, some approaches are specifically geared to be flexible and will deal with different circumstances in different ways.

Beginning with the common factors approach, Beitman's (Beitman et al., 2005; Beitman et al., 2006) future-oriented approach will be taken as an exemplar. It takes the focus on the future as the common factor that cuts across all treatment approaches. This approach is not considered suitable for acutely suicidal clients or those with problems that will be responsive to medication alone (Beitman et al., 2005). It is best used with clients who are high on reactance and internalizing in their coping mechanisms. Self-awareness is valued, as is the presence of environmental support. As for the therapist, she must believe that change is possible in order for the treatment to be maximized. If these client and therapist characteristics sound as if they would apply to many other therapies as well, that is because this is an approach that focuses on common factors.

The situation is different with technical integration, where the therapist responds to the needs of different clients with different techniques. Using Beutler's prescriptive therapy as a model (Beutler et al., 2005; Beutler et al., 2006), the approach seeks to match characteristics of the client with the types of interventions that will lead to the most beneficial results. Beutler and colleagues (2006) put it this way:

In order to select and fit particular treatments to clients, three questions must be answered: (1) what client and treatment variables
and characteristics are related to beneficial therapeutic change?
(2) What combination of client and treatment qualities best predicts
and facilitates benefits? And, (3) what are the relative contributions to
improvement of client, treatment, relationship, and client-treatment
matching factors? (p. 123)

With this approach, almost any client can be treated, but the appearance
of the treatment will vary depending on the answers to these questions.
For some clients, who are high on reactance and high on internalization,
the treatment will resemble that offered by Beitman (Beitman et al., 2005;
Beitman et al., 2006), but for others, who might not be seen by Beitman,
a very different treatment plan will be devised.

For theoretical integration, Ryle (Ryle, 2005; Ryle & McCutcheon,
2006) developed cognitive–analytic therapy to meet the needs of a large
number of clients served by the British National Health Service. It is considered suitable for most clients and is applicable to clients with conditions as varied as those with learning difficulties, eating disorders, medical
complaints in general practice, insulin-dependent diabetics, borderline
personality disorder, and psychosis (Ryle, 2005). The focus is on the therapeutic relationship, the most significant common factor in every treatment,
and not on diagnosis. However, again, the treatment can be wide-ranging
because there are adaptations to fit the particular needs of each client.

For assimilative psychodynamic integration, the treatment is rooted in
psychodynamic theory, and the clients who are suitable generally resemble
those who can be seen in more traditional psychodynamic approaches,
although the introduction of varying techniques widens the breadth of
clients who can be seen. Generally, it is most indicated with anxiety, stress-
related, mood, or personality disorders. It is less useful for clients in insti-
tutional settings or those with substance abuse, active psychosis, organic
brain disorders, or emergencies (Stricker & Gold, 2005).

The second major problem to be considered in this section concerns the therapist and the problems that might occur in learning and

applying the approach of psychotherapy integration. A psychotherapist who wants to learn psychodynamic psychotherapy must learn about psychodynamic theory and practice. A psychotherapist who wants to learn cognitive–behavioral psychotherapy must learn about cognitive–behavioral theory and practice. A psychotherapist who wants to learn psychotherapy integration must learn about psychodynamic theory and practice, cognitive–behavioral theory and practice, and much more. It is a heady and challenging route to follow.

I can best illustrate this issue with a personal reflection (for more detail, see Stricker, 2000). I was trained as a psychodynamic therapist and followed that path with some success and much confidence for many years. At the same time, I found myself incorporating other approaches (speaking prose, as illustrated in the quotation from Molière at the beginning of this book) without telling supervisors or colleagues very much about what I was doing. I did this with some added success, but also with some shame and guilt. It wasn't what I was supposed to do, and despite the evidence of my senses, it wasn't supposed to be very helpful to my clients. Whatever success I achieved was presumed to be superficial, short-lived, and countertherapeutic. That was not consistent with my experience, but it was consistent with all of my training (and with what I continued to teach my students). One of the turning points for me came when I was introduced to the Society for the Exploration of Psychotherapy Integration (SEPI) and found myself in the company of many esteemed colleagues who had the same experience (accompanied by the same shame and guilt) that I had undergone. As I became familiar with the literature in this field, both with important earlier works (Alexander & French, 1946; Frank, 1961) and stunning new ones (Goldfried, 1980; Wachtel, 1977), I found myself doing much as I had done before, but with new confidence and pride. SEPI meetings served as a reinforcement of these attitudes and a feeling of acceptability with a new and accepting reference group.

However, it wasn't as simple as being freed to do the same as I always had done. I always felt as though I was a competent psychodynamic therapist, but my knowledge of cognitive–behavioral and experiential approaches was sketchy and often inaccurate. There was much new learning to be done, both from reading and consultation with valued colleagues (supervision also would have been valuable, although I did not do that in any formal way). Some techniques that I tried were remarkably effective; others fell flat despite what the literature led me to expect. There was a need to introduce these new techniques in a manner that was seamless rather than jarring, and that took some skill that only developed slowly and with experience. I also had to learn to live with uncertainty. Psychodynamic theory was a safe haven, but this new approach represented uncharted waters. It was an exciting time, but not an easy one.

The more general expression of the obstacles that are illustrated by my personal experience is that a single school approach is most likely to be taught in graduate school and will provide a sense of having a clear roadmap. The student will feel as though there is a reassuring certainty to what must be done, and in the time of anxiety that is graduate school, certainty is welcome indeed (Gold, 2005). However, as training begins to clash with reality, and it becomes clear to the student that whatever was taught was effective but insufficient, there will be an attempt, by the conscientious student, to add the tools that will make her more effective. This will point the way to psychotherapy integration. Initially, the approach may be technical integration, as techniques are added without a clear theoretical basis for doing so. However, assimilative integration, based on whatever the home school happened to be, is a point of easy departure, and theoretical integration may lie in the future. One of the several integrative models that have been developed may be adopted, or the student may wish to develop her own unique approach.

This set of choices for the student leads to two questions. The first of these concerns training methods (Norcross & Halgin, 2005). Two principal models have been developed. The first model begins by teaching psychotherapy integration early in the training program and follows through with it consistently. The alternative is to teach individual therapeutic approaches at the beginning of the program and then use psychotherapy integration as a capstone experience to tie everything together. The first approach has the advantage of consistency throughout the training of the student. The second, which I prefer, has the advantage of giving the student comfort and familiarity with one or more specific approaches so that she then has something to integrate at the end of the program. Aside from these approaches to graduate training, some imaginative models of postdoctoral training have been developed (Beitman & Yue, 1999; O'Brien & Houston, 2000). Finally, many people who have developed individual integrative models offer workshops and other training experiences, so that the opportunities to learn psychotherapy integration abound, even if it was not part of graduate training.

This brings us to the second question for the student who is dissatisfied with traditional graduate training in psychotherapy and is seeking further knowledge. A great many choices are available, but how does the student choose among them? Other than personal comfort, is there any evidence that would favor one approach over another? That question of evidence for psychotherapy integration in general, and for specific variants in particular, is the topic that we will turn to in the next chapter.

5

Evaluation

This chapter will focus primarily on evidence as defined by the evidence-based treatment approach (Sackett, Richardson, Rosenberg, & Haynes, 1997), largely because that comprises the bulk of the extant literature. However, in doing so, it should be noted that this presents the worst case for psychotherapy integration, an approach that frequently is ill suited for a manualized, treatment-oriented, and symptom-focused research design (Stricker, 2006b). This is because psychotherapy integration is a highly flexible approach and does not have the same opportunity for prescriptive application as is seen in more standardized approaches to treatment.

RESEARCH SUPPORTING EFFICACY OF APPROACH

This research is available in much greater detail in an excellent recent summary (Schottenbauer, Glass, & Arnkoff, 2005) that, using criteria somewhat more stringent than those of a traditional evidence-based approach (Chambless & Ollendick, 2001), concluded that there was substantial support for the efficacy of psychotherapy integration in 9 studies, some support in 13 studies, and preliminary support in 7 studies. I will summarize the results by looking specifically at each of the approaches to psychotherapy integration separately.

Although it is very difficult to test the common factors approach directly, there is a good deal of inferential support for the effectiveness of the common factors. We could begin with the wide agreement that psychotherapy is effective (Lambert & Ogles, 2004), but there is a lack of evidence for the differential effectiveness of the various approaches (Wampold et al., 1997). This has produced a general statement of the "dodo bird effect" (Everyone has won and all must have prizes; Luborsky, Singer, & Luborsky, 1975), an effect that is most easily accounted for by the recognition that the key mutative elements in psychotherapy are contributed by common factors such as a sound therapeutic relationship.

There are some interesting studies, often by cognitive–behavioral therapists, that also point to the importance of common or relationship factors as underlying therapeutic success. In one study (Ilardi & Craighead, 1994), the changes that occurred in cognitive–behavioral therapy (CBT) took place in the first 4 weeks, before specific techniques were introduced, so that the foundational relationship and factors such as hope and expectation seemed to underlie the change. In another (Castonguay, Goldfried, Wiser, & Raue, 1996), also conducted by prominent cognitive–behavioral therapists and also concerned with depression, two common factors, therapeutic alliance and client emotional experiencing, were related positively to change. However, one specific factor most often associated with CBT, linking distorted thoughts to negative emotions, was related inversely to change.

Turning to technical integration, we can look at the major models that have been developed. The first, multimodal therapy, developed by Lazarus (1981), has a limited amount of empirical support, although many case histories, anecdotal contributions, and uncontrolled studies support the approach. The model of technical integration developed by Beutler (Beutler & Harwood, 2000), prescriptive psychotherapy, is based on a foundation of research and has a good deal of empirical support. The matching variables that are used in the approach were chosen on the basis of a review of the research literature, with internalizing and reactance the two with the most empirical support. Externalizing clients are better suited for CBT, whereas internalizing clients do better in psychodynamic treatment. Similarly, low-reactance clients do better in CBT, whereas high-reactance clients are better suited for psychodynamic treatment. The matching protocols then were tested against other approaches in controlled studies, and the results provided strong support for this approach (Beutler, Consoli, & Lane, 2005).

Finally, outcome-informed therapy (Miller, Duncan, & Hubble, 2005) has been classified within technical integration (and sometimes within common factors) and also has a strong empirical base. The idea of using client feedback to determine interventions is captured best in the approach of Lambert (2007). His programmatic research provides some inferential evidence for the value of asking clients about their progress and responding to that feedback. It also demonstrates the real contribution that research can make to psychotherapy, in that it does not simply validate the usefulness of psychotherapy, but instead actively contributes to the choice of interventions by the practitioner. This is similar to the use that Beutler makes of research in choosing matching variables for his prescriptive therapy, another eclectic integrative effort.

Lambert's research (2007) has been conducted for almost a decade and has amassed data from thousands of clients with varied problems seen in a large number of settings. The general design is to have clients fill out an outcome measure, the Outcome Questionnaire-45 (OQ-45), after each session. The OQ-45 measures general mental health as well as symptoms, social role functioning, and interpersonal functioning. Norms of expected change are generated according to initial level of disturbance, and each client's scores are then compared to these norms. When the client's progress falls below 85% of the normative group, the therapist is given a warning signal, and a stronger signal is given if the 90% threshold is exceeded. These thresholds accurately predict treatment failure and do so with far more accuracy than the individual therapist can achieve. Clients whose therapists receive such warning signals have markedly improved outcomes as compared to those who do not. Even greater success is achieved if the warning is also given to the client, or if the therapist is given advice as to how to alter the treatment plan. Not only does this research show the importance of the scientific process for psychotherapy, it also validates the outcome-informed therapy approach to eclectic integration. Finally, it suggests that treatment length can be determined by client progress rather than by artificially and economically determined limits. Lambert's approach is a clear embodiment of the local clinical scientist (Stricker & Trierweiler, 1995; Trierweiler & Stricker, 1998) approach to psychotherapy.

The direct evidence is somewhat less impressive for theoretical integration, although there is substantial support for some variants. For example, with cognitive–analytic therapy (Ryle, 2005; Ryle & McCutcheon, 2006), randomized controlled trials (RCTs) have shown positive effects in the treatment of asthmatics and diabetics. Uncontrolled studies have shown positive effects in the treatment of psychiatric clients, clients with borderline personality, and abuse survivors. Transtheoretical psychotherapy (Prochaska & DiClemente, 2005), an approach based on stages of change with intervention processes tailored to these stages, has produced a good deal of confirmatory research (Schottenbauer et al., 2005). For example, a meta-analysis of 47 studies (Rosen, 2000) showed large effects of sequencing processes by stage for several health-related behaviors.

The evidence concerning assimilative integration also is somewhat sparser than for the other approaches to psychotherapy integration. An experiential approach, process–experiential therapy (Watson, 2006), has produced two RCTs and several process studies supporting its utility (Schottenbauer et al., 2005). There also is support for assimilative psychodynamic integration. Strong evidence is presented by Hilsenroth and Slavin (2008), who approached comorbid depressed and borderline patients and found that a psychodynamic approach augmented by structure, support, and suggestion produced clinically and statistically significant effects. Additional support is provided in the Sheffield project (Shapiro & Firth, 1987; Shapiro & Firth-Cozens, 1990), which indicated the superiority of an exploratory–directive model over a directive–exploratory model. However, this is more a sequential than an integrated approach, unlike assimilative psychodynamic integration, and, as has been mentioned previously, proper sequencing probably depends more on the presenting problem than any strict rule of thumb would indicate.

EFFECTIVENESS WITH SPECIFIC PROBLEMS AND CLIENT POPULATIONS

There is a wide range of integrative efforts, and many of them were specifically designed to be of use with specific populations. It is more difficult to state where the approach is not effective because of this wide range. Each approach is useful with some groups and not with others, but just about every group is amenable to one integrative approach or another. I will review some of the most prominent specific approaches, along with an evaluation of their efficacy.

There have been several attempts to develop treatments for depression. Foremost among these is cognitive behavioral analysis system of psychotherapy (CBASP; McCullough, 2000), an approach that integrates cognitive, behavioral, and interpersonal approaches. It has been compared with other approaches in RCTs as well as other research designs with favorable results (Schottenbauer et al., 2005). Of particular interest, CBASP has been compared to medication, alone and in combination, and usually the combined treatment appears to be more effective than either approach taken by itself.

Borderline personality disorder also has attracted much integrative attention. The most prominent approach to this serious disorder is dialectical behavior therapy (DBT; Heard & Linehan, 2005). This integrates Western (behavior therapy) and Eastern (dialectical processes, mindfulness) approaches to healing. Several RCTs have shown the efficacy of DBT (Schottenbauer et al., 2005), and it has been expanded for work with problems other than borderline personality disorder. Mindfulness itself has been the subject of several studies with a wide spectrum of disorders, and a review of these (Baer, 2003) has been very promising. Unified therapy (Allen, 2003) is an alternative to DBT as an approach to borderline personality disorder. It is based on an integration of cognitive–behavioral, psychodynamic, and family systems approaches and seems promising, although empirical evidence is still lacking. Finally, assimilative psychodynamic integration has been identified as an approach that is particularly useful with personality disorders (Gold & Stricker, 1993). It, too, has little traditional evidence, other than the work of Hilsenroth and Slavin (2008), but a good deal of clinical application makes it appear to be promising.

Similarly, the anxiety disorders have been specifically targeted by Wolfe (2005) in an integrative effort that includes contributions from cognitive–behavioral, psychodynamic, and humanistic approaches. It, too, has little empirical support as yet, but the work is imaginative and promising.

Most of the integrative efforts have been focused on adults. Child therapy seems to be an area that is particularly appropriate for integrative work because of the manifold needs of children and the difficulty in working with them in anything but a flexible manner. However, with some exceptions (Coonerty, 1993; FitzPatrick, 1993; Keat, 1990), this is not an area of broad coverage. At the other end of the age spectrum, older adults, who also require flexibility and should be a target of integrative efforts, have not been widely studied, again with some exceptions (Papouchis & Passman, 1993).

There are other areas in which flexibility is indicated, but integrative efforts have lagged. These include work with organic disorders (Becker, 1993), chronic pain (Dworkin & Grzesiak, 1993), and severe mental disorders (Hellkamp, 1993). These have not produced a great deal of evidence and are areas ripe for further study. As much as psychotherapy integration has produced and validated, there are many areas remaining for further expansion, as well as a need to augment the findings that already have been achieved.

6

Future Developments

There have been several significant publications concerning future developments in psychotherapy integration, and I will review them in this chapter, as well as adding some additional comments beyond those that have already been published.

At the 2004 Society for the Exploration of Psychotherapy Integration (SEPI) meeting, there was a dialogue between the two founders of the society, each of whom played a critical role in the subsequent developments within the psychotherapy integration movement, Marvin Goldfried and Paul Wachtel. It was transcribed and published (Wachtel & Goldfried, 2005) to share more widely their thoughts about developments in and directions for psychotherapy integration. Much of the dialogue was a paean to SEPI, applauding the genuine and significant gains stimulated by that organization. One point of discussion was the difference between psychotherapy integration as a process or as a product. The process leads to a constant exploration of psychotherapy, whereas a product would lead to one (or many) integrative therapies, a goal that seems more desirable internationally than it is in North America. Considering this issue, I would opt for a continuing exploration with new insights and procedures being developed and no system being frozen as *the* way to do psychotherapy. However, I realize that many people are seeking a better product and are not content with continuing exploration, and this has been a topic of continuing debate.

The current *Handbook of Psychotherapy Integration* (Norcross & Goldfried, 2005a) concludes with a chapter speculating about future directions (Eubanks-Carter, Burckell, & Goldfried, 2005b). These were the product of a series of questions directed to each contributor to the *Handbook*, and the chapter summarizes the responses. A complete set of the responses also was published in the *Journal of Psychotherapy Integration* (Norcross & Goldfried, 2005b).

The issue of process versus product is listed here, with a concern that psychotherapy integration is in the contemplative stage (Prochaska & DiClemente, 2005) and should be moving toward action. This is one of the several superordinate themes that were identified in the responses to the survey. Although there is a tension between action and exploration, the field has moved toward a great deal of action, as witnessed by the myriad systems that have been detailed in previous chapters. I see more of a danger in having psychotherapy integration spawn an additional set of single school approaches than in maintaining a continuing curiosity and creative growth in developing ways of being helpful to clients. An additional point listed under this concern was the appropriate one of the need to get beyond the current research paradigm, based as it is on diagnoses as presented in the *Diagnostic and Statistical Manual of Mental Disorders* and on randomized controlled designs. There are broader dimensions available for conceptualizing clients (PDM Task Force, 2006), and it is more important, but difficult, to capture sources of variance that contribute to therapeutic change than specific interventions (Lambert & Ogles, 2004). This endorsement of research evidence in tandem with concern for the need for new research models may be an important future source of development within psychotherapy integration.

A second superordinate theme—and one with which I am in complete agreement—is the need to adopt a broader view of integration. There have been several creative attempts to integrate psychodynamic and cognitive–

behavioral approaches (with lesser attention given to humanistic approaches, at least in the United States), but this is not the only area of needed integration. There has been less emphasis on the need to integrate the findings of basic psychological science, and there are rich possibilities in the literature of cognitive science, social psychology, developmental psychology, and neuropsychology, among others. There also is a need to integrate extratherapeutic sources of influence, as psychology in general, and not just psychotherapy integration, tends to downplay important sources of influence such as social class and cultural differences. For this latter concern, the need to use more culturally diverse research participants and clients is manifest, and this also is an important dimension for future developments. In this same line of expansion of concerns, a focus on client strengths rather than an exclusive focus on psychopathology would be useful.

There are several directions in which practice should be altered, and the ultimate goal of the psychotherapy integration movement is to provide better service to our clients. Arriving at a consensus about the common factors is an important direction, as there seems to be agreement among many researchers that these factors account for the largest source of variance contributing to client change (Wampold et al., 1997), particularly when the therapeutic relationship is recognized as one such common factor. The development of a common language, free of jargon, would aid communication between groups that often do not benefit from the advances of each other, and this would be reminiscent of the pioneering work of Dollard and Miller (1950) many years ago. These would contribute to the development of manuals that might help individual practitioners and optimally would be the result of collaborations between practitioners and researchers, an effort that finally would provide an instantiation of the vaunted scientist–practitioner model (Raimy, 1950). Eubanks-Carter and colleagues (2005b) note, appropriately, that the goal of these manuals would not be to create homogenization of therapists, but rather to ease access of each therapist, developing an individual style, to the contributions of others and to facilitate appropriate referrals when therapists and clients are not well matched.

Just as developments within practice are predicted, important research developments are also identified. Among these are the need for additional attention to process research, an important change if we are to move beyond randomized control trials and more simplistic measures of interventions. Given the variance contributed by the individual practitioner, measures of therapist skillfulness also are valued. There is a very important recognition of the potential role of practice-research networks (Wolf, 2005), a source of information that truly would facilitate communication between active practitioners and productive researchers. Finally, although not mentioned in the chapter, we might look to the development of qualitative methodology (Patton, 2002) as an additional source of information about the therapeutic encounter.

In considering the future of theory, the contributors seem to agree that it is research rather than theory that holds the key to future development. The search for a grand unified theory is akin to the search for the Holy Grail, and, in my view, likely to be as unproductive. A focus on clinical strategies (Goldfried, 1980) is seen as a more productive—and more potentially integrative—path for future development than a further proliferation of theory, particularly if the theoretical musing is not grounded in research.

Within the realm of education and training, the debate remains as to whether the training program should emphasize integration from the beginning or should teach individual orientations first so that the student has something to integrate later. Regardless of the strategy adopted, respect for alternatives, and skepticism about revealed truths, is central to an integrative outlook and should be encouraged. There also is a need to remember that students prefer certainty to ambiguity (Gold, 2005), and this is an attitude that must be addressed at whatever point in training it arises. Eubanks-Carter and colleagues (2005b) come down on the side of early integration. My preference is for the alternative strategy, but there is agreement that this should be a research rather than a polemic question.

Aside from this comprehensive summary of the opinions of many leaders in the field, as defined by their contributions to the *Handbook*, there also was attention to the future at the conclusion of the *A Casebook of Psychotherapy Integration* (Stricker & Gold, 2006). Here, it was noted that psychotherapy integration itself also is undergoing an integrative process, so that the traditional categorization of integrative approaches may be giving way to blurred boundaries between these categories, leading to a need to conceptualize integrative efforts in a new way.

If the current categories of psychotherapy integration are retained, the most likely candidate for an additional category is the approach currently known as client-directed therapy (Miller, Duncan, & Hubble, 2005), and typically classified as a common factors approach (although sometimes included within technical integration). This has very impressive research support for the value of altering treatment plans based on client progress and feedback (Lambert, 2007), and also has shown some interesting clinical applications (Duncan, Sparks, & Miller, 2006; Gold, 2006).

Psychotherapy integration may treat the number of approaches to psychotherapy as a more manageable and realistic number than the widely cited 400 by recognizing the commonalities among these varied approaches. However, the actual extant number of different approaches ultimately depends on our definition of difference. For lumpers, the number will be small, whereas splitters will see more differences (Hey, 2001); whatever the number, psychotherapy integration is a creative endeavor and promises to continue to contribute in a realistic and flexible manner to the development of the psychotherapeutic enterprise.

7

Summary

Psychotherapy integration encompasses various attempts to look beyond the confines of single school approaches to see what can be learned from other perspectives. It is characterized by openness to various ways of integrating diverse theories and techniques. It can be distinguished from integrative psychology because it is a process rather than a product and characterizes an ongoing attitude toward treatment rather than an alternative to other single school approaches to psychotherapy. It also can be distinguished from eclecticism by the systematic and often theory-driven nature of the work. Eclecticism usually refers to drawing from various approaches according to the preferences and predilections of the practitioner, whereas psychotherapy integration also uses various approaches but chooses the interventions on the basis of theoretical or other systematic considerations.

The term *psychotherapy integration* has been applied to several distinctive approaches to integration. Common factors, the first approach to psychotherapy integration to be developed, identifies those aspects of psychotherapy that are present in most, if not all, therapeutic systems (Frank, 1961). This was followed chronologically by technical integration

(Lazarus, 1976), in which a combination of techniques is drawn from different therapeutic systems without any specific theoretical approach determining the selection. This approach is most often confused with eclecticism. Theoretical integration, or an attempt to understand the client by developing a superordinate theoretical framework that draws from a variety of frameworks, was the next to develop (Wachtel, 1977) and may be the most difficult to achieve of the approaches to psychotherapy integration. Finally, assimilative integration (Messer, 1992), which combines treatments drawn from different approaches but remains guided by a unitary theoretical understanding, is the most recent addition to the list of approaches to psychotherapy integration.

To develop psychotherapy integration approaches, it is helpful to view psychotherapy as being constituted of a series of theory/technique units. It is important to recognize that theory and technique are separable, so that the presentation of a particular technique in one framework does not preclude its use in another. Integration then may occur at the level of theory (theoretical integration), at the level of technique (technical eclecticism), or, more likely, at both levels (assimilative integration). As to common factors, similarities are sought at both the theory and technique level, as well as with strategies adopted by the clinician. The techniques associated with a particular theoretical approach do not present an exhaustive list of possibilities for the practitioner, as other techniques from other approaches may be introduced. However, shifting a technique from one orientation to another changes the context in which it is used and, by doing so, changes the meaning and perhaps the utility of the technique.

The most important work in the area of common factors, and the one most often cited in the psychotherapy integration literature, is the first of the landmark volumes by Frank (1961). This work was far more ambitious than simply seeking common factors in psychotherapy, as it sought to discover the common factors in all healing processes, including such concepts as faith healing and shamanism along with psychotherapy. Among the factors identified were an emotionally charged healing relationship; a healing setting; a myth based on a rational and credible conceptual scheme to explain symptoms; and a healing ritual. Certainly these are all present in psychotherapy, but they also exist in the other healing processes. The initial focus on common factors has evolved, by some investigators, into a search for common principles of change, as exemplified by the early work of Goldfried (1980) and more recent contributions by Castonguay and Beutler (2005).

The first work that might be classified as technical integration was introduced by Lazarus (1976) in the form of multimodal therapy. Lazarus refers to this as an eclectic approach, although an argument might be made that it is assimilative integration, with social learning theory providing the organizing theory and other interventions being assimilated. However, the difficulty in classification is indicative of a more recent problem, as the four categories usually employed have somewhat fuzzy boundaries. In any case, Lazarus provided an excellent example of an approach to psychotherapy that did not hold rigidly to any single orientation, but drew interventions from many orientations in developing a flexible approach to treatment.

The preparation of the field for integration came to fruition with the watershed book by Wachtel (1977), an integration of psychodynamic and behavioral thought in the first fully realized example of theoretical integration. It not only was important as a work of integration but also made psychotherapy integration an acceptable form of treatment and led to a series of works that now could be classified together rather than viewed as unconnected and discrete apostasies. Perhaps the most important aspect of Wachtel's integration was the presentation of his system, cyclical psychodynamics, which contained the notion of a cyclical rather than a linear process of causality. Thus, it was possible for insight to lead to behavior change, as psychoanalysis long had held, but also for behavior change to lead to insight, so that it was reasonable to intervene at either point to produce change.

Shortly thereafter, Goldfried (1980) presented an important article that also might be classified within the common factors area. He recognized the difficulty in achieving integration at the level of theory, which often provided incompatible formulations, or at the level of technique, which also were quite disparate. Instead, he looked for commonalities at an intermediate level that he referred to as clinical strategy. Orientations that differed widely in theory and in preferred interventions were compatible at this middle strategic level, which included processes such as providing feedback and corrective emotional experiences.

The final major class of approaches to psychotherapy integration, assimilative integration, was presented by Messer (1992). He provided the theoretical structure for this approach, which later was instantiated by works such as that of Gold and Stricker (2001). Their assimilative psychodynamic integration uses a relational psychodynamic theory as the organizing theory but incorporates interventions from CBT and humanistic–experiential theories to supplement standard psychodynamic interventions when it is indicated clinically.

To the extent that this volume pursued any single approach within psychotherapy integration, assimilative psychodynamic integration (Gold & Stricker, 2001; Stricker & Gold, 2002; Stricker, 2006a) was the approach that was developed in greatest detail. This approach relies on relational psychodynamic theory as the organizing principle but then assimilates many different technical interventions drawn from cognitive, behavioral, experiential, and systems approaches, as they may be helpful. It is interesting to note that relational psychoanalysis itself is integrative within the psychodynamic area, as it incorporates many earlier models, including object relations, attachment theory, and self-psychology. The key difference separating relational from earlier models of psychoanalytic thinking is in the conception of the content of the unconscious, with more emphasis placed on interpersonal sources than biological ones.

The three-tier model of psychotherapy and personality (Gold & Stricker, 1993; Stricker & Gold, 1988) is central to assimilative psychodynamic integration as we practice it and was presented in some detail. The three tiers can be conceptualized as a triangle divided longitudinally into three sections. The top section, Tier 1, is concerned with behavior. The middle section, Tier 2, deals with cognition, affect, perception, and sensation. The base of the triangle, Tier 3, represents unconscious processes, including images, representations of others, motives, and conflicts. Because each of the tiers relates to the other two, causality is not linear from the bottom up, as in a traditional psychodynamic model, but is cyclical, with changes in each tier reverberating within the others. Thus, changes in behavior can lead to changes in conscious perceptions and also can lead to changes in the structure of unconscious representations of the event. The implication of this circularity is that change in any tier can lead to change in the others. The model was expanded to include the relational and cultural influences on the individual.

The goals of psychotherapy integration are idiographic rather than nomothetic. Each treatment is tailored to the needs of the individual client, and each treatment therefore pursues a different set of goals as determined by the needs of the client. The therapist determines the processes and strategies necessary to reach those goals, but the goals themselves are established jointly with the client.

The full range of concerns of psychotherapy integration is captured best by a mnemonic device I devised for teaching purposes. ABCDEF represents:

Affect

Behavior

Cognition

Dynamics

Environment

Fysiology

Each of the integrative approaches goes beyond the limited focus of a single school approach and addresses more than one (and sometimes all) of the concerns highlighted by the mnemonic. There also is no suggestion of linear direction implied, and the circular model endorsed by the three-tier approach works here as well, as each of these concerns has impact on the others and reverberates throughout treatment.

One of the key concepts in psychotherapy integration is the centrality of the therapeutic relationship and alliance. Bordin (1979) has described the necessary components of this alliance as consisting of the agreement on a goal, agreement on the means of reaching the goal, and establishing a bond that will facilitate the first two of these components. Although cognitive–behavioral therapists may focus more on interventions as a means of achieving the established goal and psychodynamic therapists are more focused on the bond that exists, integrative therapists need to keep all of these components in mind as they establish a productive working relationship.

There are problems with psychotherapy integration as there are with any psychotherapeutic approach. Some of the integrative approaches are not suitable for specific types of clients, although the variability inherent in the integrative process allows for a great flexibility and latitude in adopting interventions to the needs of the client. A greater problem occurs with the task of the therapist. A psychotherapist who wants to practice psychotherapy integration must learn about psychodynamic theory and practice, cognitive–behavioral theory and practice, and often the theory and practice of other single school orientations as well. She also must deal with the anxiety that occurs when the certainty inherent in the practice of any single school approach must be abandoned for the ambiguity inherent in the flexibility of an integrative approach (Gold, 2005). Finally, there is the need to blend different approaches in a seamless manner, as interventions take on new meaning when presented in an unfamiliar context.

It probably is more realistic to think of psychotherapy integration as being a research-informed practice rather than an evidence-based practice, although several questions may be raised about the proper definition of evidence. If evidence is considered in a broad fashion, psychotherapy integration certainly can take its place without shame among the evidence-based approaches. With an appropriate expansion of research methodology to include quasi-experimental designs, qualitative research, and practice research networks, evidence would be more realistic for psychotherapy integration and for psychotherapy in general. However, even within the more narrow definition of evidence, there is considerable support for psychotherapy integration. The most comprehensive review of the research evidence supporting psychotherapy integration can be found in Schottenbauer, Glass, and Arnkoff (2005). Their review found that psychotherapy integration had substantial support in 9 studies, some support in 13 studies, and preliminary support in 7 studies.

Diversity is considered in its widest form, and includes age, gender, gender identity, race, ethnicity, culture, national origin, religion, sexual orientation, disability, language, and socioeconomic status. Although psychotherapy integration, like too many other orientations, is not fully developed in its responsiveness to the needs of this wide variety of clients, because of the flexibility and willingness to adapt to different circumstances inherent in the approach, it shows promise in being able to adjust to the needs of a variety of people. As such, it is useful with a broad and diverse set of clients.

Psychotherapy integration takes many different forms, as indeed practice itself does, but also has survived evaluation to take its place among the acceptable approaches to helping people in need. It provides an opportunity for practitioners, who long have been speaking prose, to develop a systematic framework for doing so. Psychotherapy integration is an imaginative and realistic approach and is in the vanguard of helping techniques as we move forward in the quest to deliver useful services.

Glossary of Key Terms

ACCELERATED EXPERIENTIAL DYNAMIC PSYCHOTHERAPY (AEDP)   Fosha's theoretically integrated approach that emphasizes affect rather than behavior or cognition.

ACCOMMODATION   Piaget's term for the alteration of an internal process, such as a theory of therapy; it is used as a complement to assimilation.

ACCOMPLICE   A person who plays a complementary, enabling role in a dysfunctional relationship.

ACTION-ORIENTED APPROACHES   Approaches to psychotherapy that seek to change behavior.

ALLIANCE RUPTURES   Disruptions in the therapeutic relationship.

ASSIMILATIVE INTEGRATION   An approach to psychotherapy integration that combines interventions drawn from different approaches but remains guided by a unitary theoretical understanding.

ASSIMILATIVE PSYCHODYNAMIC INTEGRATION   Stricker and Gold's assimilative integration approach, using relational psychotherapy as an organizing principle.

ATTACHMENT   The pattern of care seeking developed in infancy and reflected in adult behavior in many relationships, including the therapeutic.

BASIC-ID   An acronym developed by Lazarus referring to the areas of behavior, affect, sensation, imagery, cognition, interpersonal functioning, and drugs/biology, all necessary areas to target in integrative efforts.

BEHAVIORAL PSYCHOTHERAPY   Fensterheim's theoretically integrated approach that attempts to blend psychodynamic and behavioral work beginning with a behavioral rather than a psychodynamic foundation.

CHAIR WORK   Interventions, either with an empty chair or two chairs, that promote affective experience.

CLARIFICATION   An exploration of the meaning of a pattern of events or behaviors.

CLIENT-DIRECTED (*SEE* OUTCOME-INFORMED) THERAPY   A common factors approach by Miller, Duncan, and Hubble in which therapy is guided by the client's preferences and theory of change, supplemented by the results of the outcome of the process.

COGNITIVE–ANALYTIC THERAPY   Ryle's theoretically integrated approach that blends an object relations approach to psychotherapy with cognitive–behavior therapy.

COGNITIVE BEHAVIORAL ANALYSIS SYSTEM OF PSYCHOTHERAPY (CBASP)   McCullough's approach that integrates cognitive, behavioral, and interpersonal approaches; specifically designed for the treatment of depression.

COGNITIVE–BEHAVIORAL THERAPY (CBT)   Beck's theoretical integration of behavior therapy and cognitive science.

COLLABORATIVE EMPIRICISM   Approach in which the client and therapist formulate the client's thoughts, attitudes, beliefs, and behaviors and then design experiments to determine their validity and usefulness.

COMMON FACTORS   Approach to psychotherapy integration that identifies those aspects of psychotherapy that are present in most, if not all, therapeutic systems.

CONFRONTATION   An indication by the therapist to a client of the existence of a particular dysfunctional behavior.

CONFRONTATION RUPTURES   Disruptions in the therapeutic alliance that are marked by direct expressions of anger or dissatisfaction.

CONSTRUCTIVIST   Approach that views the perception of an experience as central to the meaning of that experience, in contrast to any inherent "real" meaning.

CORRECTIVE EMOTIONAL EXPERIENCE   Experiencing old relationships in new and more benign or supportive ways.

COUNTERTRANSFERENCE   The sum of the therapist's attitudes and affective experiences in relation to the client.

CYCLICAL PSYCHOTHERAPY   Wachtel's theoretical integration of behavior therapy and psychoanalysis, emphasizing the cyclical rather than linear nature of change.

DIALECTICAL BEHAVIOR THERAPY (DBT)   Linehan's approach, classified as theoretical integration, designed for the treatment of borderline personality disorder, which integrates Eastern and Western approaches to psychotherapy.

DIVERSITY   The consideration of factors such as age, gender, gender identity, race, ethnicity, culture, national origin, religion, sexual orientation, disability, language, and socioeconomic status.

DODO BIRD EFFECT   A consistent finding that different approaches to psychotherapy produce similar results.

DOSE-EFFECT RELATIONSHIP   The relationship that exists between the number of psychotherapy sessions and the effect of the treatment.

ECLECTICISM   An approach in which the therapist chooses interventions because they work, without regard to theory or any other reason for using techniques other than efficacy.

EGO STRENGTH   The positive personality assets that will enable the client to overcome his anxieties and to grow in psychotherapy.

EGO-SYNTONIC   Behaviors, values, and feelings that are consistent with one's ideal self-image.

EMOTIONAL CLIMATE   The quality and quantity of affective engagement and involvement between client and therapist.

EMPTY-CHAIR TECHNIQUE   The client is asked to address an empty chair in which a significant person in his life is imagined to sit, perhaps leading to the expression of feelings that have been difficult to access.

ENACTMENT   The client repeats an earlier experience, both with the therapist and in the other relationships in his life.

EVIDENCE-BASED PRACTICE   Approach that tries to specify the way in which therapists should make decisions by identifying evidence that may be relevant to practice.

EVIDENCE-BASED RELATIONSHIPS   Approach to evidence-based practice that looks at relationship factors rather than interventions as critical.

EXPECTATION VIDEO   Beitman's central concept, concerning the client's expectations of the future.

EXTERNAL VALIDITY   The ability to generalize research conclusions from the unique and idiosyncratic settings, procedures, and participants of a particular study to other populations and conditions.

GENERALIZABILITY   The ability to make inferences from a research finding to an external application of the finding.

HOMEWORK ASSIGNMENT   A task given by a therapist to a client to be performed between sessions.

IDIOGRAPHIC   A focus on the individual rather than on general norms.

INSIGHT-ORIENTED APPROACHES   Approaches to psychotherapy that seek to promote understanding.

INTEGRATIVE PROBLEM-CENTERED THERAPY   Pinsof's approach, which addresses the relevant systems that impact an individual, such as the individual, family, environmental, and self systems.

INTEGRATIVE PSYCHOTHERAPY   An established and integrated approach to psychotherapy, similar to other single school approaches.

INTERNAL VALIDITY   The demonstration of a causal relation between two variables.

INTERPERSONAL–CHARACTEROLOGICAL MODE   Approach to therapeutic data that is cognizant of the joint contributions of the client and the therapist to the interaction and that sees the present as important without discounting the influence of the past.

INTERPRETATION   An intervention designed to give previously unappreciated meaning to a pattern of behavior.

INTRAPSYCHIC–TRANFERENTIAL MODE   Approach to therapeutic data that focuses on the client's unconscious determinants that help to shape the current interpersonal relationship between the client and the therapist.

LOCAL CLINICAL SCIENTIST (LCS)   A psychotherapist who uses scientific research and methods, general scholarship, and personal and professional experience to develop plausible and communicable formulations of specific individual client presentations.

MANUALIZED TREATMENT   A treatment that is implemented based on interventions specified in a manual.

META-ANALYSIS   Approach to data analysis in which the results of several studies are combined and analyzed as if they were the results of one large study.

MINDFULNESS   Awareness of one's thoughts, actions, or motivations.

MULTIMODAL THERAPY   The approach of Lazarus, classified as technical integration and based on the use of many techniques within the framework of social learning theory.

NECESSARY AND SUFFICIENT CONDITIONS   Rogers's view that the therapist must provide conditions of empathy, genuineness, and unconditional positive regard.

NORMATIVE   A focus on general norms rather than on the individual.

ONE-PERSON PSYCHODYNAMIC APPROACH   An intrapsychic approach in which there is one active participant, the client, in the therapeutic process.

OUTCOME-INFORMED THERAPY   The use of clinical measurement tools to track therapeutic outcomes in psychotherapy and to revise treatment plans based on these findings, as pioneered by Lambert (2007).

PLACEBO CONTROL   A research comparison group that is given a treatment condition that is assumed not to have an active therapeutic ingredient.

PRECONTEMPLATIVE STAGE   One of Prochaska's stages of change, in which the client is not yet open to active efforts at change.

PRESCRIPTIVE PSYCHOTHERAPY   Beutler's approach, classified as technical integration and based on matching interventions to client characteristics.

PRIZING–SAFETY MODE   Approach to therapeutic data that emphasizes the relationship that emerges out of the interaction of two human beings without regard to distortions created or shaped by past experiences.

PROCESS RESEARCH   Research that focuses on the process of rather than (or as well as) the outcome of psychotherapy.

PSEUDOALLIANCE   The client seems to be going through the motions of doing what is asked without actually engaging in the process of therapy.

PSYCHOTHERAPY INTEGRATION   A process that looks beyond the confines of single school approaches to see what can be learned from other perspectives; it is characterized by openness to various ways of integrating diverse theories and techniques.

QUALITATIVE METHODOLOGY   Research that does not focus on statistical procedures or other means of quantification, instead using interviews and other measures of textual report; it often is hypothesis generating rather than hypothesis testing.

QUASI-EXPERIMENTAL DESIGN   A research design that lacks random assignment of participants to conditions.

RANDOMIZED CONTROL TRIAL (RCT)   A research design in which different interventions, including control groups, are assigned at random to clients.

REACTANCE   A central concept in Beutler's prescriptive approach, referring to a client's inclination to resist external influence.

RELATIONAL PSYCHODYNAMIC THEORY   A psychodynamic theory emphasizing the therapeutic relationship and development as a product of relationships.

REMA   Weinberger's identification of relationship, exposure, mastery, and attribution as the key common factors.

REMINISCENCE THERAPY   Approach introduced by Butler (1960) that involves thinking back on one's life and communicating about it to the therapist.

RESEARCH-INFORMED PRACTICE   The practitioner uses whatever research evidence is applicable, searches her experience for guidance, and keeps systematic records to identify similar situations.

SEAMLESS   The ability to move from one therapeutic stance to another without having a jarring effect on the therapeutic relationship.

SELF-WOUNDS   A concept of underlying problems with the integrity of the self that is central to Wolfe's theoretically integrated approach to treating anxiety disorders.

SEPI   The Society for the Exploration of Psychotherapy Integration, the primary organization for the field of psychotherapy integration.

SOCRATIC QUESTIONING   A therapeutic technique in which questions are asked rather than answers provided.

SYNCRETISM   Combining techniques without any systematic rationale for doing so.

TECHNICAL INTEGRATION   Approach to psychotherapy integration in which a combination of techniques are drawn from different therapeutic systems without regard for any specific theoretical approach.

THEORETICAL INTEGRATION   Approach to psychotherapy integration that attempts to understand the client by developing a superordinate theoretical framework that draws from a variety of different frameworks.

THEORY/TECHNIQUE UNITS   A concept that theory and technique are separable, and each intervention reflects both, so that the presentation of a particular technique in one framework does not preclude its use in another.

THERAPEUTIC ALLIANCE   The relationship between client and therapist, marked by a bond between them and agreement as to the goals and methods of treatment.

THIRD-PARTY PAYER   An entity other than the client, usually an insurance plan, that pays for the treatment.

THREE-TIER MODEL   Approach in which the person is conceptualized as having three tiers of experience (behavioral, conscious perceptual and cognitive, and unconscious); these three tiers interact without any fixed linear direction of influence.

TRANSFERENCE   The client viewing the therapist in part based on prior experiences with important figures from the past.

TRANSTHEORETICAL APPROACH   Prochaska's stage theory of change in psychotherapy.

TWO-CHAIR TECHNIQUE   The client is asked to imagine that one part of him is in one chair and another part in the other chair; the client moves from chair to chair as the two parts have a discussion with each other.

TWO-PERSON PSYCHODYNAMIC APPROACH   An interpersonal approach in which there are two active participants in the therapeutic process.

UNIFIED PSYCHOTHERAPY   Allen's theoretically integrated approach that attempts an integration of psychodynamic therapy with systems theory.

WITHDRAWAL RUPTURES   Disruptions in the therapeutic alliance that occur when the client disengages from the therapist, the therapeutic process, or his own emotions.

Suggested Readings

Beutler, L. E., & Clarkin, J. F. (1990). *Systematic treatment selection: Toward targeted therapeutic interventions.* New York: Brunner/Mazel. An excellent presentation of one of the major examples of technical integration.

Frank, J. (1961). *Persuasion and healing.* Baltimore, MD: Johns Hopkins University Press. The classic work that brought together the area of common factors.

Gold, J., & Stricker, G. (2001). Relational psychoanalysis as a foundation of assimilative integration. *Journal of Psychotherapy Integration, 11,* 43–58. A statement of the assimilative psychodynamic integration approach toward assimilative integration.

Goldfried, M. R. (1980). Toward the delineation of therapeutic change principles. *American Psychologist, 35,* 991–999. An early and influential common factors approach that defined the need to seek integration at a strategic rather than a technical or theoretical level.

Lazarus, A. A. (1976). *Multimodal behavior therapy.* New York: Springer. The first work on technical integration, and still one of the most influential.

Messer, S. B. (1992). A critical examination of belief structures in interpretive and eclectic psychotherapy. In J. C. Norcross & M. R. Goldfried (Eds.), *Handbook of psychotherapy integration* (pp. 130–165). New York: Basic Books. The first presentation of the assimilative integration approach.

Norcross, J. C., & Goldfried, M. R. (2005). *Handbook of psychotherapy integration.* New York: Oxford University Press. The most current compendium of works on psychotherapy integration and the source of information on every important approach.

Society for the Exploration of Psychotherapy Integration. (n.d.). Welcome to the SEPI homepage. Available at http://sepiweb.org. The Web site for the organization that provides a journal, a conference, and a professional identity for psychotherapy integration.

Stricker, G., & Gold, J. (Eds.). (2006a). *A casebook of psychotherapy integration.* Washington, DC: American Psychological Association. A presentation of cases that illustrate most of the current approaches to psychotherapy integration.

Wachtel, P. L. (1977). *Psychoanalysis and behavior therapy: Toward an integration.* New York: Basic Books. The landmark work that introduced theoretical integration and set the stage for the psychotherapy integration movement.

References

Alexander, F. (1963). The dynamics of psychotherapy in light of learning theory. *American Journal of Psychiatry, 120,* 440–448.

Alexander, F., & French, T. (1946). *Psychoanalytic therapy.* New York: Ronald Press.

Allen, D. M. (2003). *Psychotherapy of borderline personality disorder: An integrated approach.* Mahwah, NJ: Erlbaum.

Allen, D. M. (2006). Unified therapy with a client with multiple cluster B personality traits. In G. Stricker & J. Gold (Eds.), *A casebook of psychotherapy integration* (pp. 107–120). Washington, DC: American Psychological Association.

American Psychological Association. (2002). Ethical principles of psychologists and code of conduct. *American Psychologist, 57,* 1060–1073.

Anchin, J. (2006). A hermeneutically informed approach to psychotherapy integration. In G. Stricker & J. Gold (Eds.), *A casebook of psychotherapy integration* (pp. 261–280). Washington, DC: American Psychological Association.

Baer, R. A. (2003). Mindfulness training as a clinical intervention: A conceptual and empirical review. *Clinical Psychology: Science and Practice, 10,* 125–143.

Beck, A. T., Rush, A. J., Shaw, B. F., & Emery, G. (1979). *Cognitive therapy of depression.* New York: Guilford Press.

Becker, M. (1993). Organic disorders. In G. Stricker & J. Gold (Eds.), *Comprehensive handbook of psychotherapy integration* (pp. 353–364). New York: Plenum Press.

Beier, E. G. (1966). *The silent language of psychotherapy.* Chicago: Aldine.

Beitman, B. D., & Saveanu, R. V. (2005). Integrating pharmacotherapy and psychotherapy. In J. C. Norcross & M. R. Goldfried (Eds.), *Handbook of psychotherapy integration* (2nd ed., pp. 417–436). New York: Oxford University Press.

Beitman, B. D., Soth, A. M., & Bumby, N. A. (2005). The future as an integrating force through the schools of therapy. In J. C. Norcross & M. R. Goldfried (Eds.), *Handbook of psychotherapy integration* (pp. 65–83). New York: Oxford University Press.

Beitman, B. D., Soth, A. M., & Good, G. E. (2006). Integrating the therapies through their emphases on the future. In G. Stricker & J. Gold (Eds.), *A casebook of psychotherapy integration* (pp. 43–54). Washington, DC: American Psychological Association.

Beitman, B. D., & Yue, D. (1999). *Learning psychotherapy: A time-efficient, research-based, and outcome-measured psychotherapy training program.* New York: Norton.

Beutler, L. E., & Clarkin, J. (1990). *Differential treatment selection: Toward targeted therapeutic interventions.* New York: Brunner/Mazel.

Beutler, L. E., Consoli, A. J., & Lane, G. (2005). Systematic treatment selection and prescriptive psychotherapy: An integrative eclectic approach. In J. C. Norcross & M. R. Goldfried (Eds.), *Handbook of psychotherapy integration* (2nd ed., pp. 121–143). New York: Oxford University Press.

Beutler, L. E., & Harwood, T. M. (2000). *Prescriptive psychotherapy: A practical guide to systematic treatment selection.* New York: Oxford University Press.

Beutler, L. E., Harwood, T. M., Bertoni, M., & Thomann, J. (2006). Systematic treatment selection and prescriptive therapy. In G. Stricker & J. Gold (Eds.), *A casebook of psychotherapy integration* (pp. 29–41). Washington, DC: American Psychological Association.

Bordin, E. S. (1979). The generalizability of the psychoanalytic concept of the working alliance. *Psychotherapy, 16,* 252–260.

Bowlby, J. (1980). *Attachment and loss.* New York: Norton.

Bugenthal, J. F. T., & Kleiner, R. (1993). Existential psychotherapies. In G. Stricker & J. R. Gold (Eds.), *Comprehensive handbook of psychotherapy integration* (pp. 101–112). New York: Plenum.

Butler, R. (1963). The life review: An interpretation of reminiscence in the aged. *Psychiatry, 26,* 65–76.

Caspar, F. (2008). The current status of psychotherapy integration in Germany and Switzerland. *Journal of Psychotherapy Integration, 18,* 74–78.

Castonguay, L. G., & Beutler, L. E. (Eds.). (2005). *Principles of therapeutic change that work.* New York: Oxford University Press.

Castonguay, L. G., Goldfried, M. R., Wiser, S., & Raue, P. J. (1996). Predicting the effect of cognitive therapy for depression: A study of unique and common factors. *Journal of Consulting and Clinical Psychology, 64,* 497–504.

Castonguay, L. G., Newman, M. G., Borkovec, T. D., Grosse Holtforth, M., & Maramba, G. G. (2005). Cognitive–behavioral assimilative integration. In J. C. Norcross &

M. R. Goldfried (Eds.), *Handbook of psychotherapy integration* (2nd ed., pp. 241–260). New York: Oxford University Press.

Chambless, D. C., & Ollendick, T. H. (2001). Empirically supported psychological interventions: Controversies and evidence. *Annual Review of Psychology, 52,* 685–716.

Cohen, A. B. (2009). Many forms of culture. *American Psychologist, 64,* 194–204.

Consoli, A. J., & Chope, R. C. (2006). Contextual integrative psychotherapy. In G. Stricker & J. Gold (Eds.), *A casebook of psychotherapy integration* (pp. 185–198). Washington, DC: American Psychological Association.

Coonerty, S. (1993). Integrative child therapy. In G. Stricker & J. R. Gold (Eds.), *Comprehensive handbook of psychotherapy integration* (pp. 413–425). New York: Plenum.

Corsini, R., & Wedding, D. (Eds.). (2005). *Current psychotherapies* (7th ed.). Belmont, CA: Brooks/Cole–Thomson.

Dollard, J., & Miller, N. E. (1950). *Personality and psychotherapy.* New York: McGraw-Hill.

Duncan, B. L., Sparks, J. A., & Miller, S. D. (2006). Client, not theory, directed: Integrating approaches one client at a time. In G. Stricker & J. Gold (Eds.), *A casebook of psychotherapy integration* (pp. 225–240). Washington, DC: American Psychological Association.

Dworkin, R. H., & Grzesiak, R. C. (1993). Chronic pain: On the integration of psyche and soma. In G. Stricker & J. Gold (Eds.), *Comprehensive handbook of psychotherapy integration* (pp. 365–384). New York: Plenum Press.

Ellis, A. (1962). *Reason and emotion in psychotherapy.* New York: Stuart.

Enns, C. Z. (Ed.). (2004). *Feminist theories and feminist psychotherapies: Origins, themes, and diversity* (2nd ed.). Binghamton, NY: Haworth Press.

Eubanks-Carter, C. F., Burckell, L. A., & Goldfried, M. R. (2005a). Enhancing therapeutic effectiveness with lesbian, gay, and bisexual clients. *Clinical Psychology: Science and Practice, 12,* 1–18.

Eubanks-Carter, C., Burckell, L. A., & Goldfried, M. R. (2005b). Future directions in psychotherapy integration. In J. C. Norcross & M. R. Goldfried (Eds.), *Handbook of psychotherapy integration* (2nd ed., pp. 503–521). New York: Oxford University Press.

Eysenck, H. J. (1960). *Behavior therapy and the neuroses.* New York: Pergamon Press.

Feather, B. W., & Rhodes, J. W. (1972). Psychodynamic behavior therapy I: Theory and rationale. *Archives of General Psychiatry, 26,* 496–502.

Fensterheim, H. (1993). Behavioral psychotherapy. In G. Stricker & J. R. Gold (Eds.), *Comprehensive handbook of psychotherapy integration* (pp. 73–85). New York: Plenum.

Fernandez-Alvarez, H. (2008). Integration in psychotherapy: An approach from Argentina. *Journal of Psychotherapy Integration, 18,* 79–86.

Fiedler, F. E. (1950). The concept of an ideal therapeutic relationship. *Journal of Consulting Psychology, 14,* 239–245.

FitzPatrick, M. (1993). Adolescents. In G. Stricker & J. Gold (Eds.), *Comprehensive handbook of psychotherapy integration* (pp. 427–436). New York: Plenum Press.

Fosha, D. (2002). *The transforming power of affect: A model for accelerated change.* New York: Basic Books.

Foster, S. L., & Crain, M. M. (2002). Social skills and problem-solving training. In T. Patterson (Ed.), *Comprehensive handbook of psychotherapy: Cognitive–behavioral approaches* (pp. 31–50). New York: Wiley.

Frank, J. D. (1961). *Persuasion and healing: A comparative study of psychotherapy.* Baltimore, MD: Johns Hopkins University Press.

Frank, J. D., & Frank, J. B. (1993). *Persuasion and healing: A comparative study of psychotherapy.* Baltimore, MD: Johns Hopkins University Press.

Franklin, A. J., Carter, R. T., & Grace, C. (1993). An integrative approach to psychotherapy with Black/African Americans: The relevance of race and culture. In G. Stricker & J. R. Gold (Eds.), *Comprehensive handbook of psychotherapy integration* (pp. 465–479). New York: Plenum.

French, T. M. (1933). Interrelations between psychoanalysis and the experimental work of Pavlov. *American Journal of Psychiatry, 89,* 1165–1203.

Freud, S. (1905/1953). On psychotherapy. In J. Strachey (Ed.), *The standard edition of the complete psychological works of Sigmund Freud* (pp. 257–268). London: Hogarth Press.

Freud, S. (1912/1961). The dynamics of transference. In J. Strachey (Ed.), *The standard edition of the complete psychological works of Sigmund Freud* (pp. 99–108). London: Hogarth Press.

Freud, S. (1909/1961). Notes upon a case of obsessional neurosis. In J. Strachey (Ed.), *The standard edition of the complete psychological works of Sigmund Freud* (pp. 153–318). London: Hogarth Press.

Garfield, S. L. (1992). Eclectic psychotherapy: A common factors approach. In J. C. Norcross & M. R. Goldfried (Eds.), *Handbook of psychotherapy integration* (pp. 169–201). New York: Basic Books.

Gold, J. (1993a). The sociohistorical context of psychotherapy integration. In G. Stricker & J. Gold (Eds.), *Comprehensive handbook of psychotherapy integration* (pp. 3–8). New York: Plenum Press.

Gold, J. R. (1993b). An integrative approach to anxiety disorders. In G. Stricker & J. Gold (Eds.), *Comprehensive handbook of psychotherapy integration* (pp. 293–302). New York: Plenum Press.

Gold, J. (1996). *Key concepts in psychotherapy integration*. New York: Plenum.

Gold, J. (2005). Anxiety, conflict, and resistance in learning an integrative perspective on psychotherapy. *Journal of Psychotherapy Integration, 15,* 374–383.

Gold, J. (2006). Client-initiated integration. In G. Stricker, & J. Gold (Eds.), *A casebook of psychotherapy integration* (pp. 253–260). Washington, DC: American Psychological Association.

Gold, J., & Stricker, G. (2001). Relational psychoanalysis as a foundation of assimilative integration. *Journal of Psychotherazpy Integration, 11,* 43–58.

Gold, J. R., & Stricker, G. (1993). Psychotherapy integration with character disorders. In G. Stricker & J. R. Gold (Eds.), *Comprehensive handbook of psychotherapy integration* (pp. 323–336). New York: Plenum.

Goldfried, M. R. (1980). Toward the delineation of therapeutic change principles. *American Psychologist, 35,* 991–999.

Goldfried, M. R. (1991). Transtheoretical ingredients in therapeutic change. In R. C. Curtis & G. Stricker (Eds.), *How people change* (pp. 29–37). New York: Plenum.

Goldfried, M. R., & Davison, G. (1994). *Clinical behavior therapy* (expanded ed.). New York: Wiley-Interscience.

Goldfried, M. R., Pachankis, J. E., & Bell, A. C. (2005). A history of psychotherapy integration. In J. C. Norcross & M. R. Goldfried (Eds.), *Handbook of psychotherapy integration* (2nd ed., pp. 24–60). New York: Oxford University Press.

Goldfried, M. R., & Padawer, W. (1982). Current status and future directions in psychotherapy. In M. R. Goldfried (Ed.), *Converging themes in psychotherapy* (pp. 3–49). New York: Springer.

Greenson, R. R. (1967). *The technique and practice of psychoanalysis.* New York: International Universities Press.

Grencavage, L. M., & Norcross, J. C. (1990). Where are the commonalities among the therapeutic common factors? *Professional Psychology: Research and Practice, 21,* 372–378.

Hartston, H. (2008). The state of psychotherapy in the United States. *Journal of Psychotherapy Integration, 18,* 87–102.

Heard, H. L., & Linehan, M. M. (2005). Integrative therapy for borderline personality disorder. In J. C. Norcross, & M. R. Goldfried (Eds.), *Handbook of psychotherapy integration* (2nd ed., pp. 299–320). New York: Oxford University Press.

Hellkamp, D. T. (1993). Severe mental disorders. In G. Stricker, & J. Gold (Eds.), *Comprehensive handbook of psychotherapy integration* (pp. 385–398). New York: Plenum Press.

Hey, J. (2001). *Genes, categories, and species: The evolutionary and cognitive causes of the species problem.* New York: Oxford University Press.

Hilsenroth, M. J., & Slavin, J. M. (2008). Integrative dynamic treatment for comorbid depression and borderline conditions. *Journal of Psychotherapy Integration, 18,* 377–409.

Howard, K. I., Kopta, S. M., Krause, M. S., & Orlinsky, D. E. (1986). The dose-effect relationship in psychotherapy. *American Psychologist, 41,* 159–164.

Ilardi, S. S., & Craighead, W. E. (1994). The role of nonspecific factors in cognitive–behavioral therapy for depression. *Clinical Psychology: Science and Practice, 1,* 138–156.

Ivey, A. E., & Brooks-Harris, J. E. (2005). Integrative psychotherapy with culturally diverse clients. In J. C. Norcross & M. R. Goldfried (Eds.), *Handbook of psychotherapy integration* (2nd ed., pp. 321–339). New York: Oxford University Press.

Iwakabe, S. (2008). Psychotherapy integration in Japan. *Journal of Psychotherapy Integration, 18,* 103–125.

Keat, D. B. (1990). *Child multimodal therapy.* Norwood, NJ: Ablex.

Kohut, H. (1977). *The restoration of the self.* New York: International Universities Press.

Lambert, M. (2007). Presidential address: What we have learned from a decade of research aimed at improving psychotherapy outcome in routine care. *Psychotherapy Research, 17,* 1–14.

Lambert, M. J., Harmon, C., Slade, K., Whipple, J. S., & Hawkins, E. J. (2005). Providing feedback to psychotherapists on their clients' progress: Clinical results and practice suggestions. *Journal of Clinical Psychology/In Session, 61,* 165–174.

Lambert, M. J., & Ogles, B. M. (2004). The efficacy and effectiveness of psychotherapy. In M. J. Lambert (Ed.), *Bergin and Garfield's Handbook of psychotherapy and behavior change* (5th ed., pp. 139–193). New York: Wiley.

Lazarus, A. A. (1976). *Multimodal behavior therapy.* New York: Springer.

Lazarus, A. A. (1981). *The practice of multimodal therapy.* New York: McGraw-Hill.

Lazarus, A. A. (2005). Multimodal therapy. In J. C. Norcross & M. R. Goldfried (Eds.), *Handbook of psychotherapy integration* (2nd ed., pp. 105–120). New York: Oxford University Press.

Lebow, J. L. (2006). Integrative couple therapy. In G. Stricker & J. Gold (Eds.), *A casebook of psychotherapy integration* (pp. 211–223). Washington, DC: American Psychological Association.

London, P. (1964). *The modes and morals of psychotherapy*. New York: Holt, Rinehart & Winston.

Luborsky, L., Singer, B., & Luborsky, L. (1975). Comparative studies of psychotherapies: Is it true that "everyone has won and all must have prizes"? *Archives of General Psychiatry, 32,* 995–1008.

Marks, I. M., & Gelder, M. G. (1966). Common ground between behavior therapy and psychodynamic methods. *British Journal of Medical Psychology, 39,* 11–23.

Marmor, J. (1969). Neurosis and the psychotherapeutic process: Similarities and differences in the behavioral and psychodynamic conceptions. *International Journal of Psychiatry, 7,* 514–519.

Marmor, J. (1971). Dynamic psychotherapy and behavior therapy: Are they reconcilable? *Archives of General Psychiatry, 24,* 22–28.

McCullough, J. P. (2000). *Treatment for chronic depression: Cognitive behavioral analysis system of psychotherapy (CBASP)*. New York: Guilford Press.

Messer, S. B. (1992). A critical examination of belief structures in interpretive and eclectic psychotherapy. In J. C. Norcross & M. R. Goldfried (Eds.), *Handbook of psychotherapy integration* (pp. 130–165). New York: Basic Books.

Messer, S. B. (2006). Psychotherapy integration using contrasting visions of reality. In G. Stricker & J. Gold (Eds.), *A casebook of psychotherapy integration* (pp. 281–291). Washington, DC: American Psychological Association.

Messer, S. B., Sanderson, W. C., & Gurman, A. S. (2003). Brief psychotherapies. In G. Stricker & T. A. Widiger (Eds.), *Handbook of psychology: Vol. 8. Clinical psychology* (pp. 407–430). Hoboken, NJ: Wiley.

Messer, S. B., & Warren, C. S. (1995). *Models of brief psychodynamic therapy: A comparative approach*. New York: Guilford Press.

Messer, S. B., & Winokur, M. (1980). Some limits to the integration of psychoanalytic and behavior therapy. *American Psychologist, 35,* 818–827.

Messer, S. B., & Winokur, M. (1984). Ways of knowing and visions of reality in psychoanalytic therapy and behavior therapy. In H. Arkowitz & S. Messer

(Eds.), *Psychoanalytic therapy and behavioral therapy: Is integration possible?* (pp. 63–100). New York: Plenum.

Miller, S. D., Duncan, B. L., & Hubble, M. A. (2005). Outcome-informed clinical work. In J. C. Norcross & M. R. Goldfried (Eds.), *Handbook of psychotherapy integration* (2nd ed., pp. 84–102). New York: Oxford University Press.

Mitchell, S. (1988). *Relational concepts in psychoanalysis.* Cambridge, MA: Harvard University Press.

Molière. (1670/1957). *The middle-class gentleman: Le bourgeois gentilhomme* (H. Briffault, Trans.). Woodbury, NY: Barron's Educational Series.

Norcross, J. C. (2005). A primer on psychotherapy integration. In J. C. Norcross & M. R. Goldfried (Eds.), *Handbook of psychotherapy integration* (2nd ed.). New York: Oxford University Press.

Norcross, J. C., & Goldfried, M. R. (1992). *Handbook of psychotherapy integration.* New York: Basic Books.

Norcross, J. C., & Goldfried, M. R. (2005a). *Handbook of psychotherapy integration* (2nd ed.). New York: Oxford University Press.

Norcross, J. C., & Goldfried, M. R. (2005b). The future of psychotherapy integration: A roundtable [Special section]. *Journal of Psychotherapy Integration, 15,* 392–471.

Norcross, J. C., & Halgin, R. F. (2005). Training in psychotherapy integration. In J. C. Norcross & M. R. Goldfried (Eds.), *Handbook of psychotherapy integration* (2nd ed., pp. 439–458). New York: Oxford University Press.

Norcross, J. C., Karpiak, C. P., & Lister, K. M. (2005). What's an integrationist? A study of self-identified integrative and (occasionally) eclectic psychologists. *Journal of Clinical Psychology, 61,* 1587–1594.

O'Brien, M., & Houston, G. (2000). *Integrative therapy: A practitioner's guide.* Thousand Oaks: CA: Sage.

O'Leary, E., & Murphy, M. (Eds.). (2006). *New approaches to integration in psychotherapy.* London: Routledge.

Opazo, R., & Bagladi, V. (2008). Integrative psychotherapy: From Chile with love. *Journal of Psychotherapy Integration, 18,* 126–135.

Pachankis, J. E., & Goldfried, M. R. (2004). Clinical issues in working with lesbian, gay, and bisexual clients. *Psychotherapy: Theory, Research and Practice, 41,* 227–246.

Papouchis, N., & Passman, V. (1993). An integrative approach to the psychotherapy of the elderly. In G. Stricker & J. Gold (Eds.), *Comprehensive handbook of psychotherapy integration* (pp. 437–452). New York: Plenum Press.

Patton, M. Q. (2002). *Qualitative research & evaluation methods* (3rd ed.). Thousand Oaks, CA: Sage.

PDM Task Force. (2006). *Psychodynamic diagnostic manual.* Silver Spring, MD: Alliance of Psychoanalytic Organizations.

Pinsof, W. M. (2005). Integrative problem-centered therapy. In J. C. Norcross & M. R. Goldfried (Eds.), *Handbook of psychotherapy integration* (2nd ed., pp. 382–402). New York: Oxford University Press.

Prochaska, J. O., & DiClemente, C. C. (2005). The transtheoretical approach. In J. C. Norcross & M. R. Goldfried (Eds.), *Handbook of psychotherapy integration* (2nd ed., pp. 147–171). New York: Oxford University Press.

Raimy, V. (1950). *Training in clinical psychology.* New York: Prentice Hall.

Rice, L. N., & Greenberg, L. S. (1992). Humanistic approaches to psychotherapy. In D. K. Freedheim (Ed.), *History of psychotherapy: A century of change* (pp. 337–363). Washington, DC: American Psychological Association.

Rogers, C. R. (1957). The necessary and sufficient conditions of therapeutic personality change. *Journal of Consulting Psychology, 21,* 95–103.

Rogers, C. R. (1961). *On becoming a person.* Boston: Houghton Mifflin.

Rosen, C. S. (2000). Is the sequencing of change processes by stage consistent across health problems? A meta-analysis. *Health Psychology, 19,* 593–604.

Rosenzweig, S. (1936). Some implicit common factors in diverse methods of psychotherapy. *American Journal of Orthopsychiatry, 6,* 412–415.

Rotter, J. B. (1954). *Social learning and clinical psychology.* Englewood Cliffs, NJ: Prentice Hall.

Ryle, A. (2005). Cognitive analytic therapy. In J. C. Norcross & M. R. Goldfried (Eds.), *Handbook of psychotherapy integration* (2nd ed., pp. 196–217). New York: Oxford University Press.

Ryle, A., & Low, J. (1993). Cognitive analytic therapy. In G. Stricker & J. R. Gold (Eds.), *Comprehensive handbook of psychotherapy integration* (pp. 87–100). New York: Plenum.

Ryle, A., & McCutcheon, L. (2006). Cognitive analytic therapy. In G. Stricker & J. Gold (Eds.), *A casebook of psychotherapy integration* (pp. 121–136). Washington, DC: American Psychological Association.

Sackett, D. L., Richardson, W. S., Rosenberg, W., & Haynes, R. B. (1997). *Evidence-based medicine.* New York: Churchill Livingstone.

Safran, J. D. (1998). *Widening the scope of cognitive therapy: The therapeutic relationship, emotion, and the process of change.* Northvale, NJ: Aronson.

Safran, J. D., & Muran, J. C. (1996). The resolution of ruptures in the therapeutic alliance. *Journal of Consulting and Clinical Psychology, 64,* 447–458.

Safran, J. D., Muran, J. C., & Rothman, M. (2006). The therapeutic alliance: Cultivating and negotiating the therapeutic relationship. In W. O'Donohue, N. A. Cummings, & J. L. Cummings (Eds.), *Clinical strategies for becoming a master psychotherapist* (pp. 37–54). San Diego, CA: Academic Press.

Schottenbauer, M. A., Glass, C. R., & Arnkoff, D. B. (2005). Outcome research on psychotherapy integration. In J. C. Norcross & M. R. Goldfried (Eds.), *Handbook of psychotherapy integration* (2nd ed., pp. 459–493). New York: Oxford University Press.

Shapiro, D., & Firth, J. (1987). Prescriptive vs. exploratory psychotherapy: Outcomes of the Sheffield psychotherapy project. *British Journal of Psychiatry, 151,* 790–799.

Shapiro, D., & Firth-Cozens, J. (1990). Two year follow-up of the Sheffield psychotherapy project. *British Journal of Psychiatry, 157,* 389–391.

Sollod, R. N. (2005). Integrating spirituality with psychotherapy. In J. C. Norcross & M. R. Goldfried (Eds.), *Handbook of psychotherapy integration* (2nd ed., pp. 403–416). New York: Oxford University Press.

Stricker, G. (1994). Reflections on psychotherapy integration. *Clinical Psychology: Science and Practice, 1,* 3–12.

Stricker, G. (2000). How I learned to abandon certainty and embrace change. In M. R. Goldfried (Ed.), *How therapists change* (pp. 67–81). Washington, DC: American Psychological Association.

Stricker, G. (2006a). Assimilative psychodynamic psychotherapy integration. In G. Stricker & J. Gold (Eds.), *A casebook of psychotherapy integration* (pp. 55–63). Washington, DC: American Psychological Association.

Stricker, G. (2006b). RCTs and psychotherapy integration: A poor fit. In J. C. Norcross, L. E. Beutler, & R. F. Levant (Eds.), *Evidence-based practices in mental health: Debate and dialogue on the fundamental questions* (pp. 275–282). Washington, DC: American Psychological Association.

Stricker, G. (2006c). Recognizing and dealing with transference. In W. O'Donohue, N. A. Cummings, & J. L. Cummings (Eds.), *Clinical strategies for becoming a master psychotherapist* (pp. 95–112). San Diego, CA: Academic Press.

Stricker, G. (2007). Psychodynamic therapy. In N. Kazantzis & L. L'Abate (Eds.), *Handbook of homework assignments in psychotherapy: Research, practice, and prevention* (pp. 101–111). New York: Springer.

Stricker, G., & Gold, J. (1988). A psychodynamic approach to the personality disorders. *Journal of Personality Disorders, 2,* 350–359.

Stricker, G., & Gold, J. R. (1993). *Comprehensive handbook of psychotherapy integration.* New York: Plenum.

Stricker, G., & Gold, J. R. (1996). Psychotherapy integration: An assimilative, psychodynamic approach. *Clinical Psychology: Science and Practice, 3,* 47–58.

Stricker, G., & Gold, J. R. (2002). An assimilative approach to integrative psychodynamic psychotherapy. In J. Lebow (Ed.), *Comprehensive handbook of psychotherapy: Integrative/eclectic* (pp. 295–315). New York: Wiley.

Stricker, G., & Gold, J. (2005). Assimilative psychodynamic psychotherapy. In J. C. Norcross & M. R. Goldfried (Eds.), *Handbook of psychotherapy integration* (2nd ed., pp. 221–240). New York: Oxford University Press.

Stricker, G., & Gold, J. (Eds.). (2006a). *A casebook of psychotherapy integration.* Washington, DC: American Psychological Association.

Stricker, G., & Gold, J. (2006b). Overview: An attempt at a metaintegration. In G. Stricker & J. Gold (Eds.), *A casebook of psychotherapy integration* (pp. 293–302). Washington, DC: American Psychological Association.

Stricker, G., & Gold, J. (2007). Integrative therapy. In J. Lebow (Ed.), *21st century psychotherapies: Contemporary approaches to theory and practice* (pp. 389–423). New York: Wiley.

Stricker, G., & Trierweiler, S. J. (1995). The local clinical scientist: A bridge between science and practice. *American Psychologist, 50,* 995–1002.

Sue, S. (1998). In search of cultural competence in psychotherapy and counseling. *American Psychologist, 53,* 440–448.

Trierweiler, S. J., & Stricker, G. (1998). *The scientific practice of professional psychology.* New York: Plenum.

Vasco, A. B. (2008). Psychotherapy integration in Portugal. *Journal of Psychotherapy Integration, 18,* 70–73.

Wachtel, P. L. (1977). *Psychoanalysis and behavior therapy: Toward an integration.* New York: Basic Books.

Wachtel, P. L. (1993). *Therapeutic communication: Knowing what to say when.* New York: Guilford Press.

Wachtel, P. L. (1997). *Psychoanalysis, behavior therapy, and the representational world.* Washington, DC: American Psychological Association.

Wachtel, P. L. (2008). Psychotherapy from an international perspective. *Journal of Psychotherapy Integration, 18,* 66–69.

Wachtel, P. L., & Goldfried, M. R. (2005). A critical dialogue on psychotherapy integration. In J. C. Norcross & M. R. Goldfried (Eds.), *Handbook of psychotherapy integration* (2nd ed., pp. 494–502). New York: Oxford University Press.

Wachtel, P. L., Kruk, J. C., & McKinney, M. K. (2005). Cyclical psychodynamics and integrative relational psychotherapy. In J. C. Norcross & M. R. Goldfried (Eds.), *Handbook of psychotherapy integration* (2nd ed., pp. 172–195). New York: Oxford University Press.

Wampold, B. E., Mondin, G. W., Moody, M., Stich, F., Benson, K., & Ahn, H.(1997). A meta-analysis of outcome studies comparing bona fide psychotherapies: Empirically, "all must have prizes." *Psychological Bulletin, 122,* 203–215.

Watson, J. C. (2006). Resolving trauma in process–experiential therapy. In G. Stricker & J. Gold (Eds.), *A casebook of psychotherapy integration* (pp. 89–106). Washington, DC: American Psychological Association.

Weinberger, J. (1993). Common factors in psychotherapy. In G. Stricker & J. R. Gold (Eds.), *Comprehensive handbook of psychotherapy integration* (pp. 43–56). New York: Plenum.

Weinberger, J. (1995). Common factors aren't so common: The common factors dilemma. *Clinical Psychology: Science and Practice, 2,* 45–69.

Weiner, I. B., & Bornstein, R. F. (2009). *Principles of psychotherapy: Promoting evidence-based psychodynamic practice* (3rd ed.). New York: Wiley.

Weiss, J., & Sampson, H. (1986). *The psychoanalytic process.* New York: Guilford Press.

Wolf, A. W. (2005). Practice research networks in psychology. *Psychotherapy Bulletin, 40*(4), 39–42.

Wolfe, B. E. (2005). *Understanding and treating anxiety disorders: An integrative approach to healing the wounded self.* Washington, DC: American Psychological Association.

Wolpe, J., & Lazarus, A. A. (1966). *Behavior therapy techniques.* Oxford, England: Pergamon Press.

Young, J. (1999). *Cognitive therapy for personality disorders.* Sarasota, FL: Professional Resources Press.

Index

About the Author

George Stricker, PhD, is professor of psychology at Argosy University, Washington, DC campus. Prior to that, he was Distinguished Research Professor of Psychology in the Derner Institute, Adelphi University in Garden City, New York. He received a PhD in clinical psychology at the University of Rochester in Rochester, New York, in 1960 and an honorary PsyD from the Illinois School of Professional Psychology, Meadows Campus, in 1997. He has been at Argosy University, Washington, DC campus since 2004, and was at Adelphi University between 1963 and 2004, where he served as dean of the Derner Institute. Dr. Stricker is a diplomate in clinical psychology and was elected as a Distinguished Practitioner in Psychology. He received the American Psychological Association (APA) Award for Distinguished Contributions to Applied Psychology in 1990; the APA Award for Distinguished Career Contributions to Education and Training in Psychology in 1995; the National Council of Schools and Programs of Professional Psychology Award for Distinguished Contributions to Education and Professional Psychology in 1998; the Allen V. Williams, Jr. Memorial Award from the New York State Psychological Association in 1999; the Florence Halpern Award for Distinguished Professional Contributions in Clinical Psychology from the Society of Clinical Psychology (Division 12 of APA) in 2002; the Bruno Klopfer Lifetime Achievement Award from the Society for Personality Assessment in 2005; and the Wellner Memorial Award for Excellence as a Senior Health Services Provider in Psychology in 2005 from the National Register. He also received the Karl Heiser Award for Advocacy in 1996 from the American Psychological Association (APA). He has been president of the Division of Clinical Psychology of APA, the Society for Personality Assessment, the New York State Psychological Association, and the National Council of Schools of

Professional Psychology. He was on the board of directors of the Council for the National Register of Health Care Providers and has served on several APA boards and committees, including the Board of Educational Affairs and the Board of Educational Affairs Advisory Council on Accreditation. He also served as chair of the APA Ethics Committee. Dr. Stricker is the author or editor of about 20 books, about 30 book chapters, and more than 100 journal articles. His most recent books are *A Casebook of Psychotherapy Integration* (with Jerry Gold), and *The Scientific Practice of Professional Psychology* (with Steven Trierweiler). His principal interests are psychotherapy integration, clinical training, ethics, and research in grandparenting.